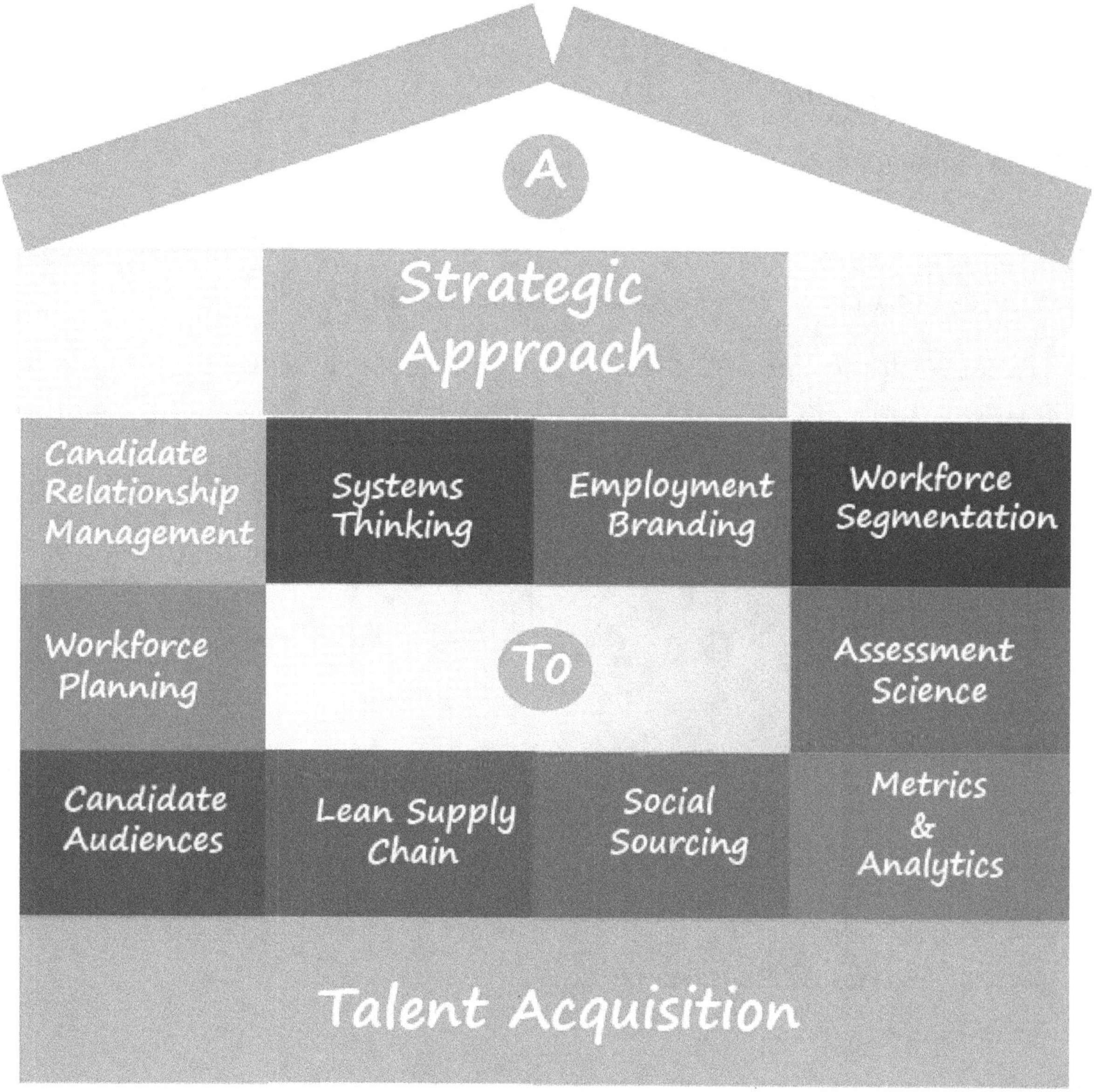

A

Strategic Approach

Candidate Relationship Management	Systems Thinking	Employment Branding	Workforce Segmentation
Workforce Planning	**To**		Assessment Science
Candidate Audiences	Lean Supply Chain	Social Sourcing	Metrics & Analytics

Talent Acquisition

Table of Contents

Disclaimer

The author and publisher of this eBook and the accompanying materials have used their best efforts in preparing this eBook. The author and publisher make no representations or warranties with respect to the accuracy, applicability, fitness or completeness of the contents in this eBook. The Information contained in this eBook is strictly for education purposes. The author and the publisher disclaim any warranties (expressed or implied), merchantability, or fitness for any particular purpose. The author and publisher shall in no event be held liable to any party for any direct, indirect, punitive special incidental or other consequential damages arising directly or indirectly from any use of this material, which is provided "as is", and without warranties. The author and publisher do not warrant performance, effectiveness or applicability of any sites listed or linked in this eBook. This eBook is copyrighted by Pradeep Sahay and is protected under

About the Author

A Talent Acquisition leader with extensive background in recruiting & selection interspersed with experience in leading Sales, P/L operations and HR generalist role(s) in diverse Industry verticals, including Technology, Telecom, Engineering/Infrastructure, and Financial Services, in both Corporate & Professional Services environment. Pradeep has led recruiting engagements, co-managed as RPO assignments for leading companies, including global brands, such as ST Microelectronic – India, Etisalat – UAE, Telsim – Turkey, Churchill Insurance (now Royal Bank of Scotland, IDC), Schneider Electric India, among others. He helped these brands scale up from start-up phase to high growth business units in their respective India & Overseas geographies. He is a keen follower of new and emergent technologies around recruitment & talent management and likes to contribute on topical issues in Talent Acquisition including integrating with Talent Management and authors a blog around process, practices & trends that are continuing to impact the recruiting industry. Published online & in print journals by Silicon India, EmeraldInsight.com, LinkedIn.Com, mosaicHUB.com

What People Have Said About Pradeep Sahay

We were planning to automate talent acquisition solution. I enjoyed Pradeep's ability to see through end-to-end resource hiring cycle and identify process bottlenecks... _Sunil Malhotra, Vice President, NIIT Technologies_

I liked working with Pradeep due to his professional focus and ability to get results. However, I came to appreciate his leadership style — strategic thinking, empathetic yet firm decision making, strong ethics and rigorous follow through when we worked closely on transforming talent management strategies and practices at four group companies... _Manoj Khare, Partner National Care Organization._

Pradeep has this unique ability to focus on the overall candidate experience at various touch points in the recruiting process. The same reinforced the employer attractiveness and value proposition enabling an informed decision. A talent acquisition strategist par excellence I would rate him high for his relationship capital... _Prem Swarup, General Manager & Global Practice Head – Business Intelligence, Wipro Technologies, USA_

Working and interacting with Pradeep is a delight – any engagement with him is intellectually stimulating. Pradeep can be credited with nurturing and growing some of the strongest client relationships Datamatics developed in the IT space in Delhi. A slow charming smile hides a sharp intellect that is always looking to bring in innovative changes. He has an unending thirst for knowledge and learning, an eye for detail and very good networking skills – traits that qualify an excellent search professional... _Sumitra Char, Senior Vice President, Datamatics Ltd_

Pradeep is a great business partner, in meeting talent acquisition requirements. Pradeep distinguishes himself by being pro-active, upfront, dependable and a go-getter. He has immense commitment and respect for his partners. His social network and understanding of the talent pool greatly supplement his personal attributes. Despite being an external partner, Pradeep is very supportive of innovative and cost beneficial delivery models which make the relationship more value-adding... _Azfar Hasib, Director HR, Cavium Networks, USA_

Buying Professional Services is rarely a comfortable experience. Unfortunately there seem to be very few professionals who can "hit the ground running" and provide the kind of professional support you need. When we associated with Pradeep as our Professional Service provider, we did not buy into a service, we bought ourselves a relationship - a top drawer Professional Services provider who had the right skills and urgency in recruiting the right person for our organization. The key is - the right kind of attitude & desire to help meet the unique manpower challenges of a rapidly growing organization. As a client he has earned my trust and confidence... Amit Gupta, Director & Mentor at Fabence.com, ex Managing Director Royal Bank of Scotland, IDC

Pradeep displayed a professional mind and he could focus on the critical and explain it to the client with empathy. This helps in making informed and effective business decisions... Emmanuel David, Executive Vice President and CHRO, Volta Ltd (A Tata Group Company)

Pradeep attended Lean Six Sigma workshop conducted by me in 2012. I appreciate his ability to relate softer intangible human resource challenges with quantitative decision making approaches. He was able to provide valuable inputs during the training on how data driven decision making can be instrumental for HR professionals. It helped other participants to see that HR equally needs efficient processes, not just words. I truly appreciate these inputs and thank him for attending the workshop... <u>Dr Shantanu Kumar,</u>

<u>Director, Benchmark Six Sigma</u>

Acknowledgements

> " We are like dwarfs standing upon the shoulders of giants, so able to see more farther than those before us."
>
> Bernard of Chartres, circa 1130

I take this opportunity to acknowledge those who have made a visible difference to my chosen vocation and have lent to me their strong shoulders on which I stand. People who are true practitioners of the 'art' and 'science' of recruiting and have helped elevate the professional standards of our Industry. People whose nuggets of wisdom, insights and inspirational words, pointed the way ahead to script this body of work. To that extent I have stolen from others but as a student of my professional craft I also understand that nothing comes from nowhere. All professional work builds on what came before. Nothing is completely original. It's right there in the Bible:

> "There is nothing new under the sun."
> Ecclesiastes 1:9

When it comes to those who have most profoundly influenced my recruiting knowledge and expertise there is none I esteem more, or feel a deeper sense of solidarity with, than Adarsh Matta. An Industry thought leader of stature, over the years he has been my strongest supporter and critic in equal measure and has never ceased to illuminate the trail I now follow by his perspicacity and sense of pragmatism. However, his greatest impact cannot ultimately be measured because in writing this book, I have so liberally, and with permission, borrowed from him.

Throughout the course of my professional career I have been fortunate to have benefited from sage heroes of our industry like Subhash Bhatia, (late) Deepak Bhargava, and to count among my friends passionate votaries like Azfar Hasib, Rajinder Bisht, Sumitra Char, Captain Kaushik, Manoj Khare and Rajiv Sharma who's boundless energy and constant contributions to our profession fans the embers of my creativity. My learning, unlearning and re-learning curve in writing this book has also benefited by following the writings and works of some brilliant strategy & recruitment practitioners such as Prof. Jacinto. C Gavino, Dave Mendoza, Shally Steckerl, Raghav Singh and Glen Cathey.

If this fraternity from my professional world has been contributory in shaping the roadmap of my career journey, the gas for the road was provided by my wife Shalini. Since the start of my recruiting career with a traditional staffing firm, her presence around me has been elemental. A constant companion through the highs and lows of my professional journey,

14

navigating the rough and tumble of a recruiter's life without her companionship would have been a daunting task. She continues to provide the revitalizing salve that protects me from permanent damage, and selflessly administers the guidance that steers me back to sanity after I lose my way including keeping me on track with projects like writing this book.

To all the people I have stolen from and to everyone else who has taken a moment to share with me an idea, suggestion, question, critical comment, challenge, or an opposing point of view, this book is dedicated to your success.

1 Foreword

Blue Ocean Strategy

Today's most competitive marketplace isn't technology but talent and a Strategic approach to Talent Acquisition (TA) will even be more crucial as markets continue to grow and change the dynamics of competition. New challenges are emerging that lessen the relevance and value of current managerial experience and knowledge. The talent that led to today's success will no longer be enough to lead organizations in the new competitive landscapes that are emerging.

Pradeep's book on TA is a welcome and timely source of knowledge and practical advice for staffing leaders and recruiters, who need to confront the changing spectrum of TA work. This book brings together in a comprehensive manner various frameworks of thought and action that help in identifying priority areas of growth and development in TA. At the same time, it explains various frameworks in a way that allows us to put them together in an integrated and coherent manner. Pradeep's approach allows us to address the real issue of cross functional collaboration in TA.

What makes this book practical and useful is by the example of a real application as a corporation works towards its own solutions in TA. The field applications of various frameworks give life to the ideas presented and show the manager how these ideas actually work in practice. Organizations looking to up the ante as they compete for talent in a VUCA environment will find the well-grounded practical insights of immense value in creating their own "Blue Ocean Recruiting" models.

Brilliantly engaging, Pradeep's book shows how TA can be a competitive advantage because of his deep experience and competence in this field, combined with his continuing willingness to listen and learn from others.

I am immensely pleased to see how Pradeep is eager and capable to share

his knowledge and wisdom with others. I am sure Pradeep will continue to

make a significant impact in the organizations and talents he encounters

Jacinto C. Gavino, DPA
Washington SyCip Graduate School of Business
AIM - Manila, Core Faculty

2 Executive Summary

Circa 2010 ... ABC, a USD 1.5 Billion diversified business group with interests spanning the Infrastructure, Power, EPC, Waste Management & the Pharmaceutical domains, was at the cusp of a major transformation, which if negotiated well would catapult the group to a USD 5 billion entity by 2015. However, global economic uncertainty was unleashing a wave of unprecedented challenges for the world economic order and organizations such as ABC could no longer take the liberty to underutilize their own capabilities. While this was one side of the coin, the other side of the coin, held out great promise to the ABC group to realize their economic and growth ambitions by maximizing on its existing capabilities. Its innovative business model required that the very best talent be sourced, engaged, developed and retained. Having a great model was hard enough; finding outstanding talent to execute it was even more challenging, particularly in the markets where the group operated. The top leadership was unanimous in its thinking that putting the right talent in the right roles at the right time would be the key differentiator that would keep the group out in the front, ahead of its rivals. The leadership at ABC also understood that there is a difference between applying nominal improvements to talent acquisition and truly **optimizing** the function to boost strategic impact. This backdrop, in light of a changing business landscape and the marketplace opportunities, reinforced the need to re-orient the focus of ABC group's Talent Acquisition strategy from its present state of a tactical, reactive process to a strategic program capable of consistently sourcing, recruiting and on-boarding the best talent. The central challenge here was to synthesize, identify, and leverage dispersed capabilities within the TA discipline.

Organizations typically create capabilities through utilization of resources at multiple levels. Optimization is about ensuring effective and efficient deployment of existing resources for capability maximization and is the result of interplay between utilization, efficiency and effectiveness. The

Exhibit(s) below graphically portray this linkage as also the key triggers at

ABC group towards creating an optimized Talent Acquisition function

Utilization
It is the proportion of the available time (expressed as a %) for which the resources are deployed

Efficiency
It is the ratio of the output to the input of the resources

Effectiveness
It is the extent of the match between the actual outcome and the intended outcome of the resources

Ideal state optimization results with the concurrent maximization of utilization, efficiency & effectiveness

High Utilization

High Efficiency

High Effectiveness

Source: Optimizing the Organization, Subhash Khare, Tata Mc-Graw Hill Publishing Company Ltd (2006)

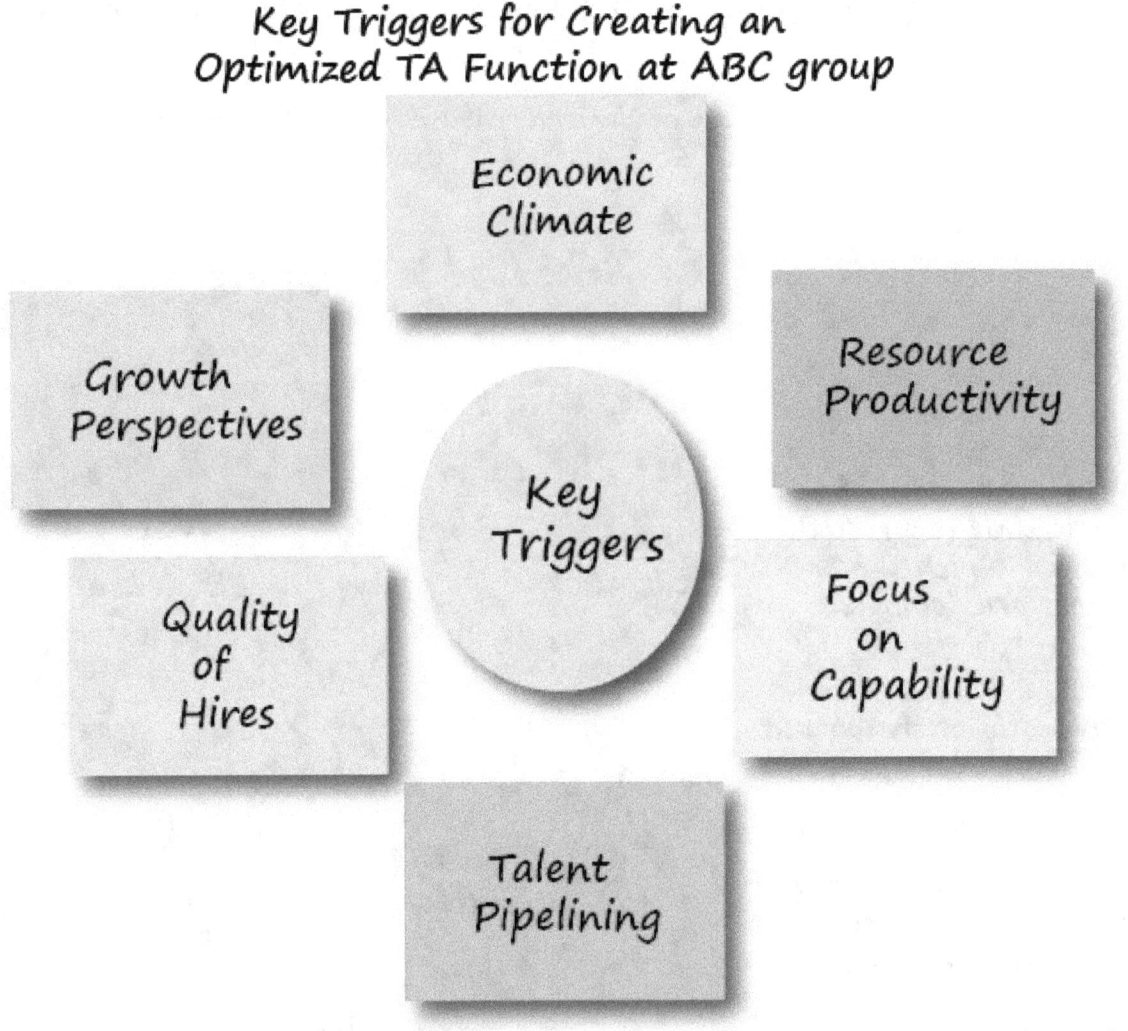

Key Triggers for Creating an Optimized TA Function at ABC group

Economic Climate

Resource Productivity

Growth Perspectives

Key Triggers

Quality of Hires

Focus on Capability

Talent Pipelining

Source: Adapted from KPMG India Analysis

Exploring & leveraging the key avenues of optimization requires the right leadership intent. Key stakeholders within ABC group were cognizant of the fact that they may not be able to sustain the envisaged optimization effort without investing to change the mindset of people. The effort would require a radical departure from the normal ways of working within the organization and also impact the work profile of individuals, teams, functions and the organization at large. A fundamental dilemma of strategy making is to reconcile the forces for continuity and for change – to focus efforts and gain operating efficiencies on the one hand, yet adapt and maintain currency with a changing business climate on the other. As, _Ecclesiastes_ reminds us, there is a time to sow and a time to reap and the leadership imperative for creating the fundamental traction for change at ABC was implicitly clear here. As pattern recognizers, these leaders understood that time was opportune to encourage new strains to displace the old crop of strategies.

The key avenues of the Talent Acquisition optimization effort at ABC included employment brand, process re-design for efficiency, technology integration, workforce planning, skill alignment, operating model & structure. This process of optimizing recruiting from a traditional relationship model to a business process model was aided by **learning from and adapting to the best practices of high impact business functions** such as lean supply chain, analytics, process re-engineering, sales & marketing among others. Some of these leading-edge interventions by the ABC' group in this transformation process are detailed in the Exhibit(s) below

Key Interventions

1 – Managing Change in creating an optimized TA Function

Measurement & Analysis Phase	Engagement Phase	Delivery Phase
Change Leadership Who is responsible?	**Stakeholder Management** How do we manage stakeholder resistance?	**Modifying Systems & Structures** How will it be measured? What are the systems implication of change?
Business Case & Vision for Change Why do it? & What will it look like when we are done?	**Involvement Strategies** How to be get buy-in from stakeholders?	**People Transition & Workforce Effectiveness** How do we help position the workforce to adopt future state business models
Change Risk Analysis What org risks need to be factored?	**Mobilizing Committment** Who else needs to be involved?	**Benefit Realization & Sustainable Performance** How do we measure & monitor progress to sustain change?

II – Recruitment Process Life Cycle Mapping

Tapping into the Voice of the Customer

Included all stakeholders across the recruitment value chain. In-depth interactions with hiring managers, employees and candidates was followed by a comprehensive mapping of existing structure, processes, systems, their relationship and interdependency to identify what was occuring and the interrelationships between the processes

Time Study of all Recruiter and Administrative Processes
as a first step in reducing time-to-fill

An Overview of Benchmark Best Practices & Key Process Elements

To serve as a foundation for creating a "Talent Acquisition - CoE" staffing infrastructure

Assessment & Mapping of all Technology Investments
To enable the required efficiencies

Roll Out of the TA CoE Model

Done in a "Trojan Horse" fashion, phase-wise over a 12 month period This was done to ensure proper alignment and integration with key affected constituents and to mitigate resistance that often accompany such change interventions in HR

Developing a Talent Pipeline	›	Based on Supply Chain Concepts
Building TA Strategy Construct	›	Based on Systems Thinking Concepts
Building a Stronger Employer Brand	›	Based on Organizational Brand Portfolio Concepts
Building Stronger HM Relationships	›	Based on Customer Service Models
Performance Monitoring & Measurement	›	Based on Sales/Marketing Metrics
Localizing TA Strategy	›	Based on Cross - Cultural Communication Model

These interventions presented an interesting data milieu and insights, which were then analyzed and implemented upon to shape the future contour of ABC' recruiting process and the required strategy outlook to achieve the business case. This interesting journey of ABC group chronicled in this

eBook attempts to articulate the challenges and the response options that confront organizations as they compete for Talent in the fast changing business climate. The initial sections of this book provide a macro view on the changing workscape and how trends & developments around technology and innovations of recent years are impacting the discipline of Talent Acquisition. I designed this eBook as a Case Study profiling the benchmark recruiting best practices and strategies of a leading Infrastructure group in India, but please bear in mind, every organization is different. The advice and strategy discussed here is by no means a 'one-size-fits-all' approach. Hopefully this text will elevate awareness and discourse on the subject and help concretize a roadmap for corporate' looking to design and implement forward looking talent acquisition strategies and move along the continuum toward best-in-class.

3 The Changing Talent Landscape – A Macro View

"A rising tide lifts all boats." - John F. Kennedy

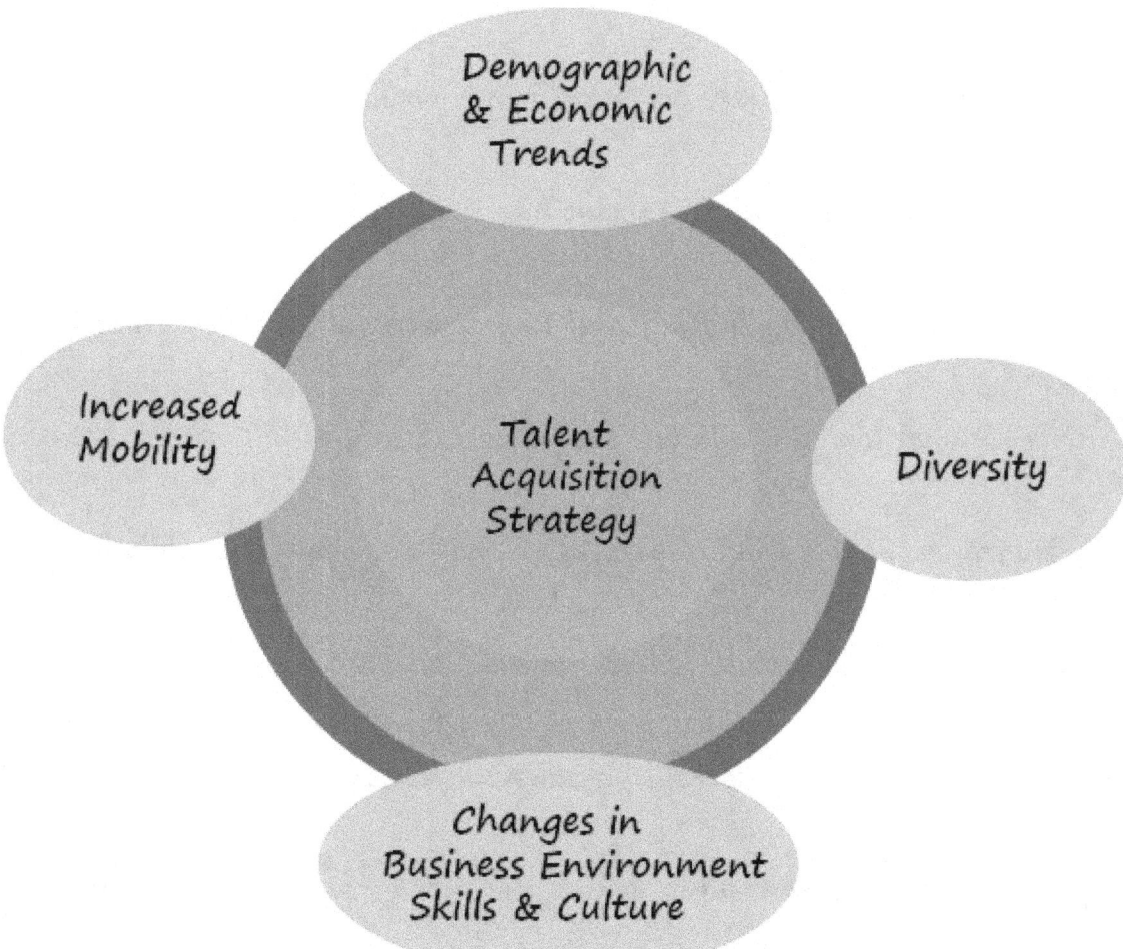

As the World Economy continues in its struggle to move ahead from the

backyards of recent financial meltdown, dramatic changes fuelled by

technology, globalization, demographics & workforce behavioral dynamics are forcing businesses to strategically adapt to new ways to fill talent scarcity gaps. Given the recessionary climate & talent imbalances in the world, organizations today are getting innovative in the way they are engaging with talent. There is increasing realization that being more innovative in sourcing and recruiting can give them a sustainable competitive advantage by finding and hiring more of the right people who can drive innovation throughout the organization. While the increasingly VUCA environment we find ourselves in has changed the global business landscape, the forces that drive talent acquisition remain in place. Companies must continue to rely on talent as a core foundation for growth and productivity. At the same time, the need for advanced, specialized talent and leadership will continue to provide challenges for enterprise recruiting efforts.

The structural labor shortage worldwide is changing the way CEO's think about the management of Talent and 'Strategic Talent Acquisition' is being increasingly seen as the fulcrum impacting all Talent Management Practices.

The real importance of talent acquisition, and the door-opener for talent management at the proverbial seat at the boardroom table, is the **recognition that a business cannot grow without the right talent. Just as importantly, businesses cannot reach the right talent without making a conscious strategic effort to do so.** As the global economy expanded dramatically between 2002 through 2007, business leaders and human resource managers worried about the intensifying international competition for talent; impact of not having the right people in place to lead and confront business challenges; as well as employing below- average candidates "just to fill positions" (Economist, October 2006; Price & Turnbull, 2007[1]). Reflecting these concerns, Price Waterhouse Cooper's 11th Annual Global Survey2008 showed that 89% of the CEOs surveyed put the 'people agenda' as one of their top priorities (PWC, 2008a,b:35[2]). Will

---

[1] The Economist, 2006, Survey: talent.'' The Economist'' from http://www.economist.com,

[2] Price Waterhouse Coopers,2008a, The 11th Annual Global CEO Survey, PWC, New York (

most companies be ready for the next economic upturn in terms of executive talent? Not if they continue to follow their present unstructured and ineffective approach to recruitment aver M/s Boris Groysberg, Nitin Nohria & Claudio Araoz[3]. In their seminal report **'The definitive guide to recruiting in good times and bad'**, they highlight that the "Future success of a vast majority of companies would depend on a complete overhaul of their recruitment practices. We need a culture of professional recruitment and retention, in good and bad times, especially in bad ones."

E & Y in its 2008 "Global HR Risk Survey" findings concluded that Talent acquisition & management was seen as the HR risk considered to have the greatest impact on the organization and the most likely to occur. Justifiably so the last few years has seen an incredible shift in how organizations source

---

September)

[3] Claudio Araoz, Boris Groysberg and Nitin Nohria, The definitive guide to Recruiting in Good Times and Bad, Harvard Business review, May'2009.

32

and hire for talent. The recruiting methodologies and approaches that businesses used in the past are being replaced by new strategies, tools and metrics that are measurably generating high quality candidates.

The **Exhibit** below captures some of the key elements of the Talent Acquisition framework gaining foothold in the lexicon of Talent decision makers.

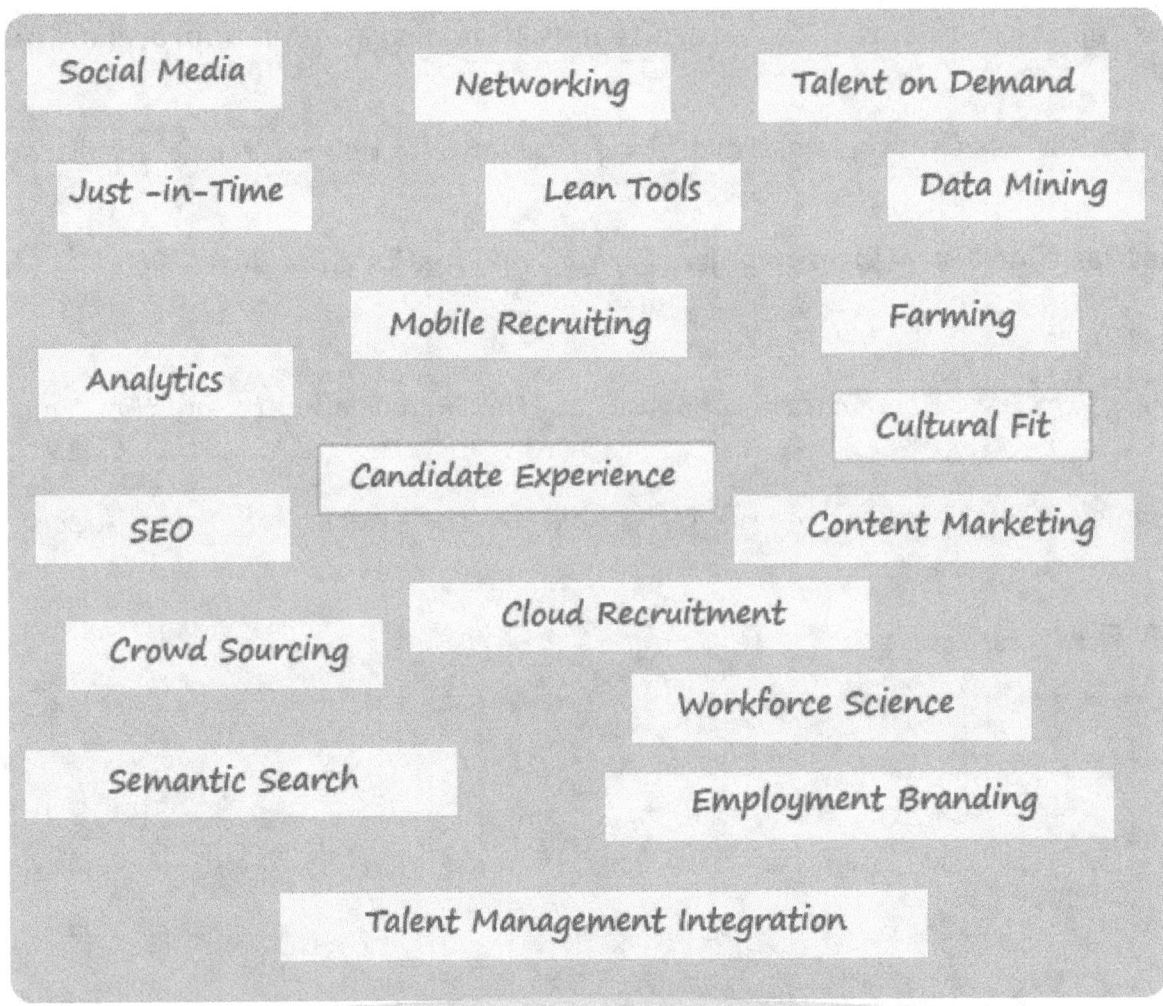

New Vernacular of High Performance
Talent Acquisition

We are today living in an age of global connectivity. Using Ulrich's[4] terms, the **talent war** represents the drive to find, develop, and retain individuals, wherever they are located in the world

Talent War

What attributes define these top performers

How do we attract the people who will best help an organization succeed

How do we integrate and retain them

---

[4] Ulrich D.2006. The Talent Trifecta. Workforce Management 32-33 (September 10)

The **Figure**[5] below delineates the talent response dimensions[6] being embraced by forward thinking organizations to attract and effectively engage talent for complex and relationship driven work.

---

[5] The Global War for Talent, Schon Beechler, Ian C. Woodward, Journal of International Management, Fox school of Business, Temple University
[6] Ibid

Global Trends

Demographic
Economic Climate
Globalization

Mobility
People
Organizations

Business
Transformation

Knowledge
Economy
Relationship Mgmt
Leadership
Challenges
High Value Skills
&
Roles

Diversity
Cultural
Generational
Gender
Working Modes

Dynamic
&
Pervasive
changes

Talent War

Talent Quality
&
Quantity

Attract
Develop
Motivate
Retain

Talent
Solutions

Scarcity Response

Aggressive Hiring
Direct Competition
Diversity Mgmt
Cyclical
Downsizing
Functional HR
Top Talent
Obsession

Creative Response

Global Mindset
Learning Agility
Broad & Deep
Talent
New & Adaptive
Systems
Diversity Leverage

The Talent response dimensions underscore the pivotal role Talent Acquisition plays in providing a foundation for all Talent Management practices. Optimizing the discipline can pave the way for a positive impact across the talent management spectrum from workforce planning to performance management, learning management, succession planning & compensation. The Key challenge here is to evolve recruitment models which can connect with Talent at large and achieve significant results in terms of cost, efficiency & business impact.

Moving ahead from the 'big picture' view the section(s) below provide an appreciation on the changing contours of the recruiting function and the evolving role and skill set of the modern recruiter in this passage of change.

4 21st Century Recruiting – From Transaction to Transformation

Recruitment has become Complex Difficult and Strategic

Recruitment today is finally moving away from transactional thinking and beginning to understand how to better connect and engage with relevant talent prospects. While the foregoing chapter threw some light on the macro-environment which is changing the recruitment landscape, the sections below delineate key trends & emerging practices that would continue to shape the future character and complexion of this discipline.

Recruitment is, and will remain a people centric function but its future promise to provide competitive advantage would lie more at the intersection of people with business, process, technology and organization strategy

A   **Talent Spotting**

Figure A

As the business environment becomes more volatile and ambiguous, and the market for top drawer talent gets tighter, the business of recruiting and sourcing is probably undergoing a paradigm shift. The biggest challenge for today's recruiter is that the job of finding talent has become more complex. In his ground breaking book It's Not the How or the What but the Who,

<u>Claudio Fernández-Aráoz</u> succinctly traces the shifting paradigms of Talent spotting, from the era of focus on physical attributes, moving on to IQ – verbal, analytical, mathematical, and logical cleverness – to the 'competency & skills' movement we see today.

He further argues that in a volatile, uncertain, complex, and ambiguous environment of today, competency-based appraisals and appointments are increasingly insufficient and organizations must navigate to a new era of Talent spotting – one in which our evaluations of one another are based not on brawn, brains, experience or competencies, but on **potential**. Geopolitics, business, industries, and jobs are changing so rapidly that we can't predict the competencies needed to succeed even a few years out[7] .

The lesson: Recruitment models of today must factor this new imperative & identify and onboard people by moving into the deeper waters of understanding a potential hire(s) psychology and motivation

---

[7] **The Big Idea – 21st- Century Talent Spotting, Claudio Fernández-Aráoz, HBR , June 2014**

Figure B

Big Data in recent times has been increasingly gaining a foothold in the

lexicon of Talent decision makers. For much of the last few years there was

talk of just what Big Data is, how it would affect talent acquisition and

talent management, and how to work with the constant and much larger

flow of data slated to have an impact on the Industry. Big Data, according

to most major analysts, is all set to change everything about what we do and why we do it in the near future. Nobody knows for certain what the future holds, but as Neil Griffiths, wrote in his introductory note in a seminal White paper by Dave Mendoza; 'it seems the coming years will see the rise of what we call Futurecasting: the ability to interrogate 'big data' generated by the increasingly 'social' digital world, and to begin basing hiring strategies and tactics on the new insights that are created.' The business world today is grappling with a deluge of data points from myriad sources. This data comes from everywhere: browsers, posts to social media sites, digital pictures and videos, purchase transaction records, tablets and cell phone GPS signals to name a few. All this data supposedly offers unprecedented awareness of people's actions and attitudes. Every day, we create 2.5 quintillion bytes of data – so much that 90% of the data in the world today has been created in the last two years alone and the number is doubling every 40 months or so. Given this ocean of data, the prevailing wisdom is centered round the great competitive advantages big data potentially offers because it allows companies to make better predictions and smarter decisions. We can target more effective interventions, and can do so in areas that so far have been dominated by gut and intuition rather than by data and rigor. But data is the lowest level of abstraction from which information is derived and the ability of Big Data to enable informed decision making can only be brought to fruition if data aka 'meaningful data' is analyzed and interpreted in the right business context. Skeptics might also question here the potential offered by big data in getting good candidates to respond when the recurrent theme song for most recruiters finds an echo in the 1988 single by the Moody Blues'. The first part reproduced below sums it up pretty well[8].

---

[8] "Every Step You Take, Every Move You Make, I'll Be Watching You – Big Data and Recruiting ", by Raghav Singh; ere.net, Dec 21, 2012

> "I know you're out there somewhere
> Somewhere, somewhere
> I know I'll find you somehow
> Somehow, somehow
> And somehow I'll return again to you."
> THE
> MOODY
> BLUES

Can Big Data Change this Tune?

Hopefully yes, but this requires a new way of thinking with a focus on trying to find new ways to find and engage candidates. As the tools and philosophies of big data spread, they will change long-standing ideas about the value of experience, the nature of expertise, and the overall practices in recruiting. Big Data innovation presents talent acquisition with a unique opportunity to raise its profile as a strategic business partner. Strategic sourcing, improved workforce planning, building critical talent pipelines, are just few of the yet many un-researched possibilities presented by applying Big Data principles to the talent acquisition process. The Industry is in consensus that the data interplay will change the nuances of recruiting as we understand now, but many are not sure how. The challenges are enormous, yet it is a transition that recruiting must engage with today. The scenario brings to mind the Chinese curse: _"May you (talent acquisition) live in interesting times."_

C   The Digitization of Recruitment

Figure C

There was a time, not so long ago, when recruiting was very much simpler. You had an approved opening and you filled it. The technology tools at our disposal included a phone, a rolodex, and a notebook. Quality candidates were plentiful and sourcing meant calling people on that rolodex, searching through one's privately maintained databases and maybe getting the word out about open positions through print publications. The recruiters 'world of data' largely revolved around the Holy Grail metric – Cost per Hire and a company's 'recruitment strategy' meant knowing when to step down on its in-house efforts and call in the third-party brigade. Hireology, a leading Talent Assessment firm in the US, recently released an [INFOGRAPHIC] titled "The Evolution of Finding Candidates", which provides an interesting account of how recruitment and selection has evolved over time. Starting with employee referrals dating back to ancient Rome, the infographic includes statistics and facts about how the industry has changed and where it is headed. Back in those "dark ages" candidates snail-mailed typewritten resumes in response to these print ads. An early innovation here was the 'fax machine' which allowed candidates to digitally send resumes to employers. But the real game-changers were the desktop computers and the advent of the internet which completely democratized recruiting. Flash

Forward to Circa 2014... times have certainly changed. Today, there are multiple layers of technologies, tools, partners and services embedded in the recruiting processes, unmatched in complexity and sophistication from the days of yore. This interplay of social media tools, video, big data, analytics, cloud based products and mobile recruiting platforms is creating an *interesting potpourri* of resources geared to enhance the recruiters' ability to more efficiently match job seekers with the right opportunities. However, digital convenience comes at the expense of meaningful engagement as digital transactions substitute physical interactions – and the trust and relationship capital they build, which is centric to the logic of the recruiting function. The challenge for the recruiting function here is to **face the implications of digital change**: in particular the loss of control over the candidate relationship, increased competition and threat of commoditization, and the need to engage digitally with all key stakeholders in the recruiting value chain. This rapid pace of digitization and the rise of the millennial generation is re-defining established workforce paradigms and will require the recruitment function to enable innovative efficiencies in its business/operating model, while creating seamless and consistent engagement with all stakeholders.

D Recruiting Revisited - The New Recruitment Models

For all the flak the recruitment function receives from Industry experts and business stakeholders, there are a lot of very talented, intelligent, and skilled individuals in the recruiting field. Second, there are some definite, emerging trends in terms of how progressive companies are re-orienting their recruiting teams. And third, there are lessons to be learned from the innovative best practices and operating models of some world-class recruiting organizations. A sneak peek at the new recruiting models of today point towards some innovative trends profiled in the

Exhibit(s) below

Enterprise Talent Acquisition Models

Outsourced

* Multiple Companies Supported
* Recruiter Team Work
* Process Ownership and accountability
* Standard Reporting & Metrics

Generalist

* Employee Relations Critical
* Limited Recruiting Experience
* Position Volume Varied
* Various reports/metrics
* Individualistic recruitment
* Multiple job responsibilities

Centralized

* Dedicated Staff
* Recruiter Team Work
* Standard Processes
* Standard Reports/Metrics
* Direct Line Reporting
* Shared Position Volumes

Decentralized

* Various roles participating
* Localized, dispersed processes
* Position Volumes varied
* Various reports & metrics
* Individualistic recruitment
* Consensus voting with participation optional

Business Alignment

Specialization Mix in the Recruiting Team

Sales Person	Metrics Manager	Workforce Planner
Business Partner	Recruitment Technologist	Social Media Expert
Community Builder	Marketer	Content Manager

Many Hues of a Recruiters Role

Hunter
Specialized Targeted

Strong Social Networking

Relationship Capital with External Candidates

Farmer
General area of discipline

Harvest Candidates from broad categories of qualified profiles

Sous Chef
Aligns efforts with overall business

Understands broad resource objectives

Strategic Alignment of talent and business

Centralization over Decentralization

Economies of scale consideration weigh significantly in centralization decisions. But another equally important factor is expertise and excellence. While not a one-size-fits-all approach, a centralized recruitment model presents organizations with a consistent hiring experience for all stakeholders and at the same time elevates the efficiency of their recruiting processes.

Closer Alignment with Business Units

In companies with several different business units, creating dedicated recruiting teams that specifically support those business groups helps them anticipate the needs of each business and find ways to develop talent pipelines that better match their future direction.

Specialization

The complexity surrounding the recruiting function today has significantly impacted a recruiter's role all geared towards how recruiting teams support their business partners & align their efforts towards achievement of business goals. Progressive organizations are finding value in dividing up the responsibilities and focus of their recruitment function around specialist areas like direct sourcing, workforce planning, hiring process management, talent analytics and recruitment marketing to name a few. Specialization is also helping the cause of the recruiting profession by creating multiple, viable career paths and helping attract top drawer talent to the recruiting industry.

Rise of Direct Sourcing & Networking

The trends driving today's recruiting marketplace are creating special challenges for organizations in the way they attract and engage with talent. The shift we are seeing here is one of moving away from the model of **attracting & selecting** the best talent to one of **attracting, engaging & selecting** the best talent. Advances in recruitment technology have been a key enabler in directing organizational focus on activities that add the most value. The near ubiquity of ATS/ CRM tools and automation of various parts of the recruiting life cycle is placing more time at the disposal of recruitment teams. The implication here is a greater emphasis on identifying top talent through direct sourcing, networking and mass-customized recruiting approaches to fit high-value recruiting targets. Sourcing, relationship-building and selling processes have to be central to the candidate engagement process. The complexity and the dynamics inherent in the recruitment process today make it imperative to view this function as a long cycle process, not a short term intervention. This requires a big picture view and close collaboration with other talent management functions (development, retention, technology substitutes, and internal movement) to ensure a focus on talent solutions, not recruiting alone...

Those who understand this will be the winners in the 21st century

5 Developing a Long Term Perspective while focused on Delivery

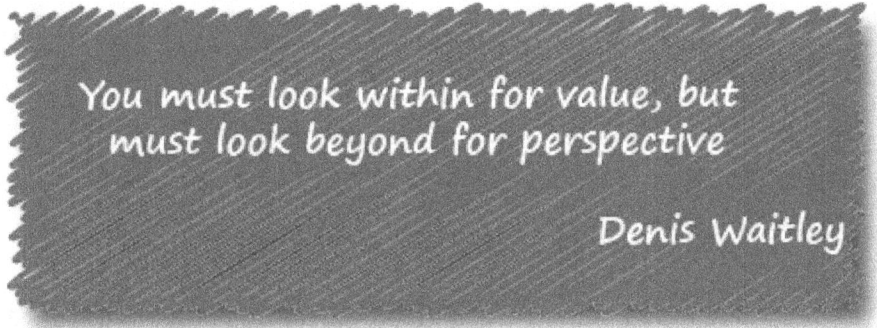

You must look within for value, but must look beyond for perspective

Denis Waitley

Figure D

While most companies recognize the importance of strategic talent operations, there are usually pressing operational issues that demand immediate attention. Lacking a strategic talent focus, organizations end up sacrificing their workforce planning capability and find themselves unable to create leadership capital due to a less than optimal talent acquisition function. When we think of it, a combination of current operating needs and the long-term business plan is integral to shaping the overall talent acquisition program. A misalignment here only ensures that the organization loses out to its competitors in the "War for Talent."

However breaking the cycle of short-term talent thinking is not easy.

Improving talent acquisition is a process of continuous evolution. This continuous improvement will be essential, because in a market where talent is a core business asset, recruiting is more than an overhead function; it is a critical capability that will drive the success of the business as a whole.

Given the sheer complexity of today's talent operations

How does an organization such as ABC identify and prioritize the options for improving performance & staying competitive?

How should it go about creating the right alignment between the strategic goals of the business & the efforts of its talent acquisition function?

If we agree that the mission of talent acquisition is to effectively staff the organization to solve business problems, support the pursuit of new business opportunities, and enable competitive advantage than an opportunity exists to assess how effectively the organization is resourced. An assessment of the current state of ABC' talent operation – talent philosophy, brand, structure, resources, and technology, was considered a *necessary first step* in designing a high business impact Talent Acquisition Strategy. The primary differentiator of this strategy, as the chapters to follow unravel, was the leveraging of concepts, tools and methodologies from other successful business systems like supply chain, sales, marketing, process reengineering & systems thinking. By leveraging the fundamental precepts of these high-priority business functions & tools, ABC group was able to significantly improve its recruiting processes and elevate its recruitment function to new heights of efficiency and effectiveness with a visible bottom-line impact.

6 Talent Acquisition at ABC Group – A Historical Perspective

Among India's largest integrated Infrastructure & Waste Management Organizations, the major operations of the group were conducted through the following group entities:

ABC Infrastructure
ABC Estates & Construction
ABC Environmental Sciences
ABC Power
ABC Pharmaceuticals

In the real-world business environment, recognizing the need for improvement and acting on it resemble two hostile clans. Resources are tight and making a strategic impact in the face of pressures to reduce recruitment costs is an ongoing challenge. The scenario confronting ABC, on one end, was the need to invest in changes needed to compete for talent in the future and on the other end, concerns around the low productivity of resources and the declining quality of hires which were having a direct impact on its key business metrics. The **Figure below** details the top pressures in talent acquisition[9] facing ABC group in the background of an increasingly competitive business environment.

Top Pressures in Talent Acquisition – ABC Group

Shortage of critical skills available in the labor pool

Pressure to meet organization growth objectives

Trouble sourcing enough qualified candidates to fill strategic roles

As an aspiring **best-in-class infrastructure player**, the stakeholders at ABC knew well that the group's talent acquisition strategy had to be the primary vehicle for driving their strategic initiatives and growth perspective. So, when it came to competing for talent, it was natural for its business leaders

---

[9] ABC Company Source

to ask, "What are other companies doing"?, "How well are we doing in relation to our peers"?, "How strong is our Employment Brand"?, "Are we creating innovative efficiencies in our recruitment practices"?, or "Are we still planning, waiting to do so in the future"?, "What are our constraining factors to onboard top talent"?. Their thoughts were well seconded by a research study conducted <u>by "The Aberdeen Group"</u> in the fall of 2013 which highlighted the distinguishing characteristics of <u>Top Strategies for Talent Acquisition between "Best-in-Class" companies and "Others"</u>. Please refer **Exhibit below**

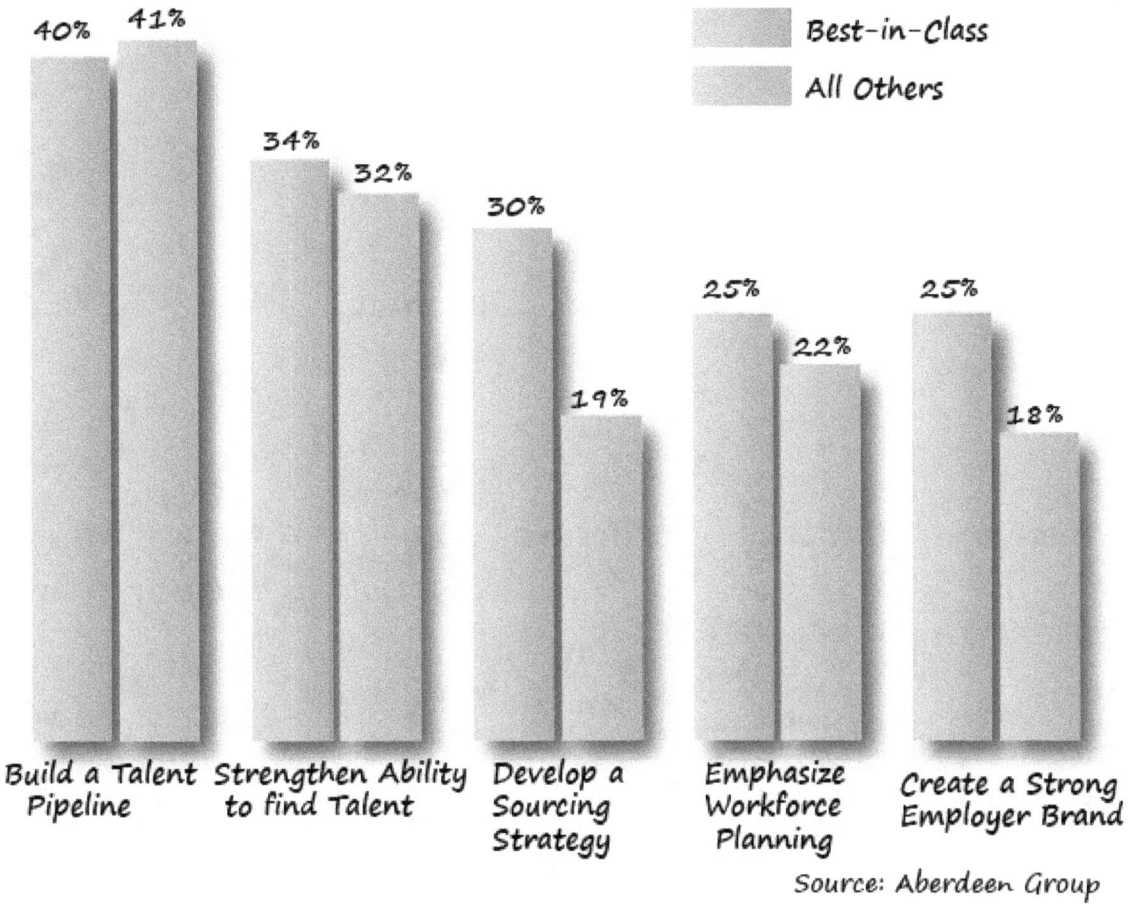

40% 41%

34% 32%

30%

25% 22%

25%

19%

18%

Best-in-Class

All Others

Build a Talent
Pipeline

Strengthen Ability
to find Talent

Develop a
Sourcing
Strategy

Emphasize
Workforce
Planning

Create a Strong
Employer Brand

Source: Aberdeen Group

To get a ground up view on these issues, the entire Talent Acquisition function at ABC group was examined through a **Strategic Framework of five primary areas. The** following section highlights the **salient aspects of this framework,** which helped identify the gap areas and the desired future state to ensure strategic business alignment.

6.1 A Strategic Framework for Talent Acquisition at ABC Group

Framework Construct

Brand	Strategy	Structure	Process & Technology	Metrics & Measurement
Stakeholder Perception	Alignment to Business Goals	Operating Model & Structure to support Execution	Process Efficiency & Technology Integration	ROI of the TA Function

How does a corporate such as ABC begin evolving its talent acquisition function to boost strategic impact? The process of optimization began by **asking questions** and knowing how to look at the function as a whole around the key elements of the **above strategic framework**. The combined framework served as a ready template to assess ABC group's current talent operations, with each of the elements presenting a common set of improvement challenges that would determine the success of its talent operations in the context of its business operations. The section(s) below delve in detail into the salient aspects of the framework elements.

6.1.1 Brand

It is important that the Employment Brand or the Employment Value Proposition (EVP) of an organization match the expectations of its targeted talent. The <u>Corporate Leadership Council</u> describes employment value proposition as "The set of attributes the labor markets and employees perceive as the value they gain through employment to an organization."

Companies with highly engaged employees articulate their values and attributes through "signature experiences" – visible distinctive elements of their work environment that send powerful messages about the organization's aspirations and about the skills, stamina and commitment employees will need in order to succeed there. An aligned EVP is important for a very simple reason: if an organization does not reasonably meet the values and the expectations of its employees and the talent it seeks, it is less desirable as a place to work. That may result in fewer quality candidates and possibly higher turnover for employees after they are on board.

The key poser before stakeholders at ABC group in initiating a realistic assess of their Employment Brand Proposition was:

> " Are we appealing to the aspirations, underlying motivations and values of talent we have and that we wish to reach out to?"

A signature experience must be buttressed by processes that send consistent messages to both present and prospective employees. The salient aspects considered important to be addressed by the key stakeholders at ABC are detailed in the Exhibit below

A	Determine the attributes most preferred and valued by our employee population
B	Understand the visible, distinctive elements of our organization's overall employee experience Do we provide a "signature experience" that tells the right story about our company
C	Understand how our employees percieve the company's ability to deliver on the preferred attributes
D	A comprehensive understanding of the talent segments who will be productive in our company in the long term. What kind of skills should they have?
E	A well-defined, well-communicated signature experience that conveys for potential hires and reinforces for employees the attributes and values of the organization
F	Understand if our benefits and perks program are aligned to our Brand Promise

This EVP construct helped reveal actionable and detailed insights to the

ABC team in formalizing a cohesive Employment Brand, which was pivotal

to its success in talent acquisition optimization effort.

6.1.2 Strategy

A business's talent acquisition strategy is both a plan and pattern of behavior for creating and sustaining advantages in the markets where it competes to attract, engage and onboard key talent. The strategy establishes a match between what an organization is capable of doing to meet business talent needs within the universe of what it might do given the constraints and opportunities in the employment market-place.

The starting point for any organizations Talent Acquisition strategy is its overarching business strategy. Business strategies are after all, the atmosphere in which a TA strategy breathes. From Talent Acquisition's vantage "getting" the business strategy definition means thinking, questioning, and translating business strategies into talent issues, needs, objectives, and strategy initiatives for meeting those objectives. For instance, if the organization goals include cutting costs, then its talent acquisition strategy should seek ways to cut agency spend, change or renegotiate terms with external partners, increase recruiter productivity, reduce attrition or apply other cost optimization strategies. If the company is looking at expansion in new markets, geographies its talent acquisition strategy must bear a localized character to create the desired talent outreach.

The following section delves into the basic building blocks of the systems thinking framework which was employed at ABC in understanding the big picture view and the structural forces affecting the contours of its TA strategy.

" Begin at the beginning," the king said gravely," and go on till you come to the end; then stop."

Alice in Wonderland
Lewis Carroll

This timeless adage embodies the construct behind **Systems Thinking**[10] - a discipline for seeing the wholes. It is a framework for seeing interrelationships rather than things, for seeing patterns of change rather than static "snapshots."

The real leverage in most business situation lies in understanding dynamic complexity not detail complexity[11]. Improving quality of hire, optimizing on costs and resources and satisfying key stakeholders through demonstrated

[10] The Systems Thinker, Vol 7, No 3, Colleen P Lannon; 1996 Pegasus Communications, Inc, Cambridge, MA

[11] Senge, Peter M. 1990, Fifth Discipline: The Art and Practice of the Learning organization, Newyork

business value in a sustainable manner was a dynamic situation confronting the ABC group. This scenario required seeing interrelationships rather than linear cause-effect chains and seeing processes of change rather than snapshots as the group went about the task of creating the right alignment between its business goals and the TA strategy.

Causal Loop Diagrams: The Essentials

Within the systems thinking framework, Causal Loop diagrams, can be thought of as sentences that can be constructed by identifying the key variables in a system (the nouns) and indicating the causal relationships between them via links (verbs). A causal loop diagram consists of four basic elements: the variables, the links between them, the signs on the links (which show how the variable are interconnected), and the sign of the loop (which shows what type of behavior the system will produce). By representing a problem scenario or issue from a causal perspective, one can become more aware of the structural forces that produce puzzling behavior.

To help understand the interplay of factors that would effectively align the TA strategy with the overarching business goals of the organization, the ABC team leveraged a causal loop construct Exhibited below

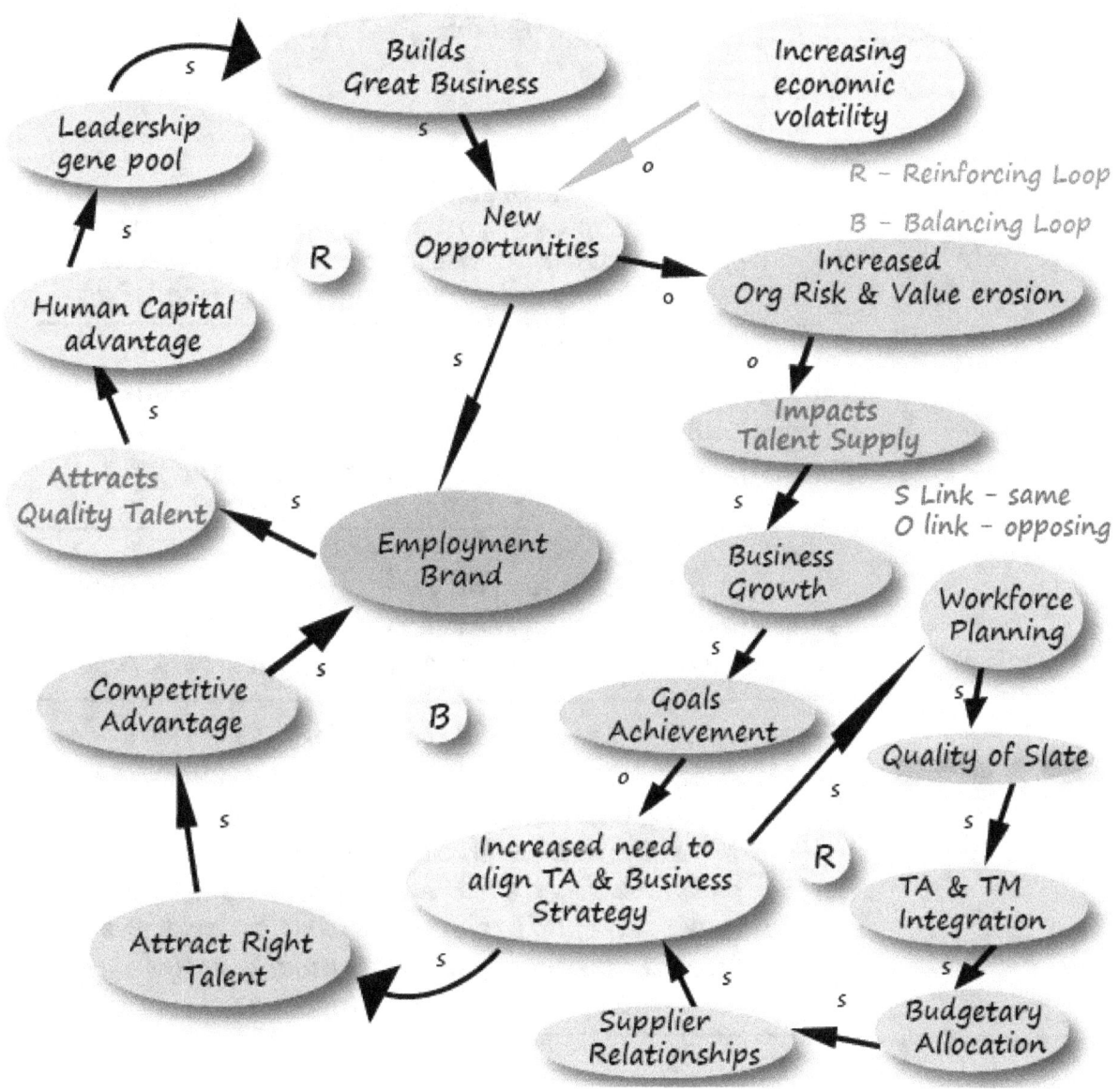

Beyond the connection to the business goals, this framework helped the ABC

team drill down on the **key areas that would drive success for their talent**

acquisition strategy. This was followed by asking pertinent questions around

them such as outlined in the following Exhibit

A	**Workforce Planning** How mature is our workforce planning capability? Does it provide us the critical ability to take action early on upcoming talent needs?
B	**Talent Supply Chain** How adept are we at building & mantaining pre- and postemployment relationships to create "just-in-time" talent reserves instead of "just-in-case" talent inventories?
C	**External Partners** Are we engaging the right types of partners, such as recruitment service and assessment providers with the required quality of service?
D	**TA & TM Integration** How well integrated is our Talent Acquisition strategy with other Talent Management practices in the organization? Do enabling links exist among efforts to source screen, select, develop, and deploy and the performance competencies required to implement business strategy objectives

A diagnosis of each of the above areas using the causal loop diagrams was

considered a necessary next step. It helped draw clear interrelationship

patterns and initiate changes wherever required. For a better appreciation the diagnosis exercise in one of the key success area ~ "TA & TM

Integration", is illustrated here. Detailed interactions with team members &

stakeholders across the TM value chain revealed a less than optimistic

picture and that something was inhibiting progress towards realizing

greater coordination of efforts and integration among the constituent units.

The CLD construct in the diagram(s) below delineates the interrelated issues

and the recommended leverage areas to improve the integration effort

CLD – I

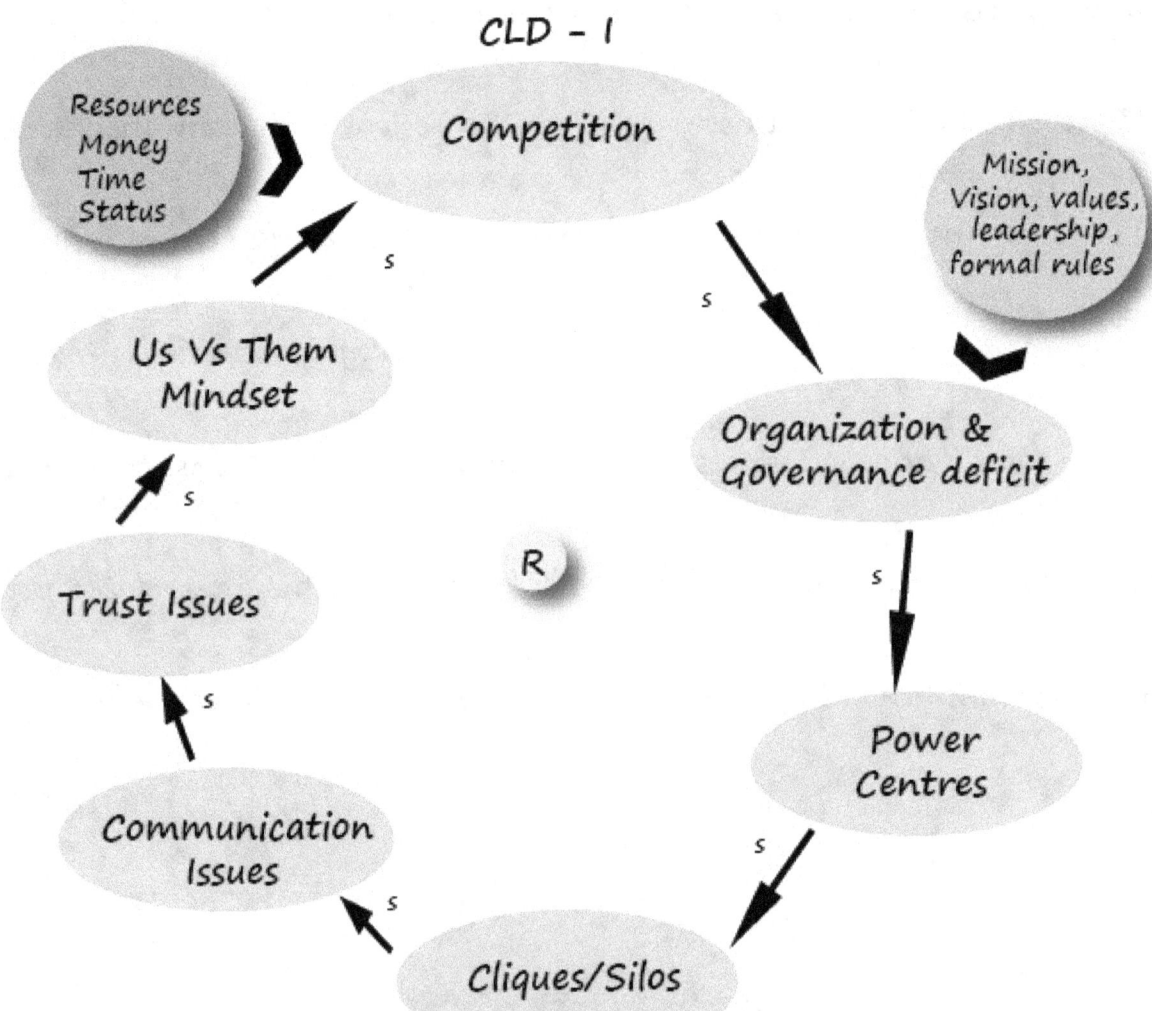

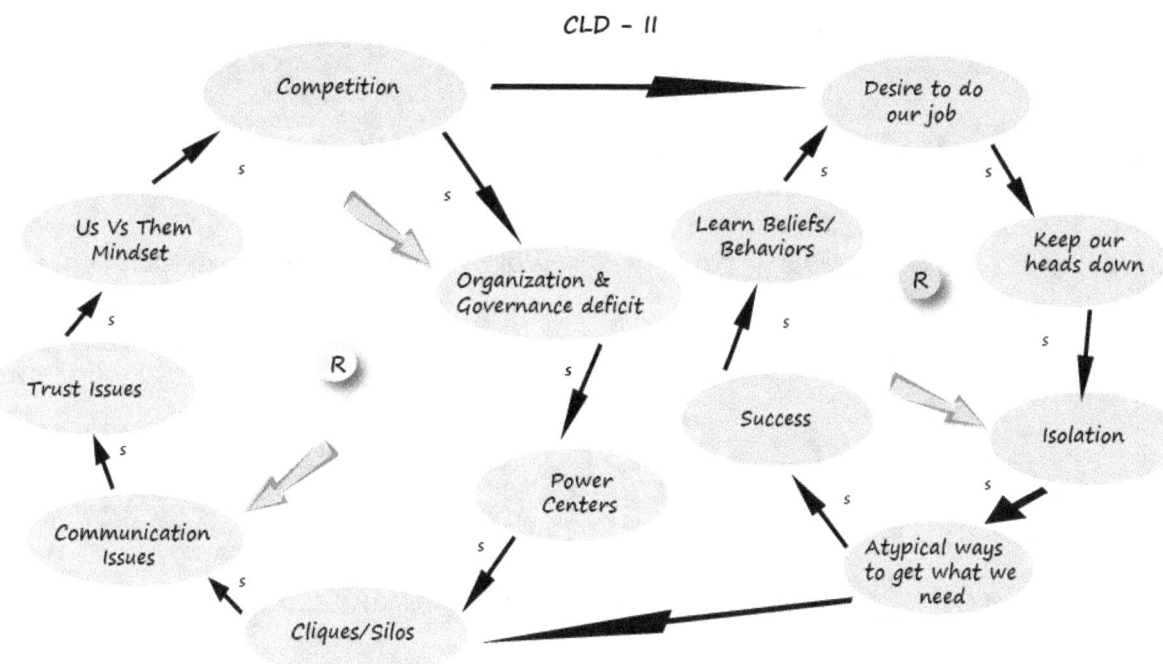

The recommended leverage areas from the above causal loop diagrams included:

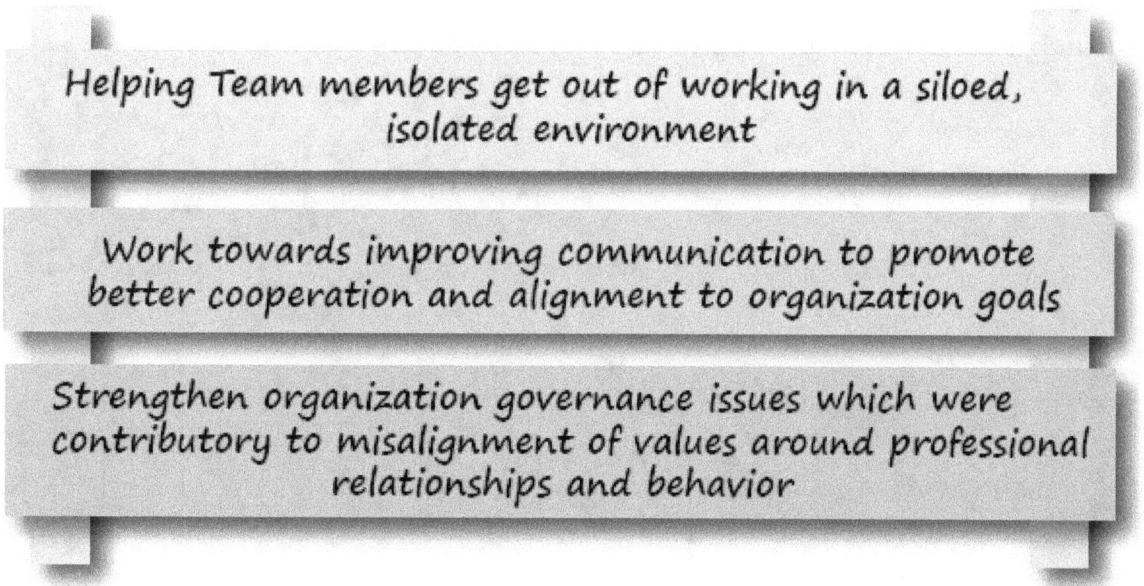

Helping Team members get out of working in a siloed, isolated environment

Work towards improving communication to promote better cooperation and alignment to organization goals

Strengthen organization governance issues which were contributory to misalignment of values around professional relationships and behavior

These causal loop constructs contained no judgment of what was right or wrong. They provided the coherence of relevant factors, the dynamic patterns over time. While strategy is a word that is usually associated with the future, its link to the past is no less central. As _Kierkegaard_ once observed, life is lived forward but understood backward. Organizations may have to live strategy in the future, but they must understand it through the past.

The reasoning & the leverage areas that followed by applying the systems thinking approach equipped ABC better to determine & shape the complexion and content of its talent acquisition strategy.

6.1.3   Structure

An operating model as the **Exhibit below** illustrates, dictates where and how the critical work gets done across an organization. It serves as a vital link between a company's strategy and the detailed organization design structure that it puts in place to deliver on strategy.

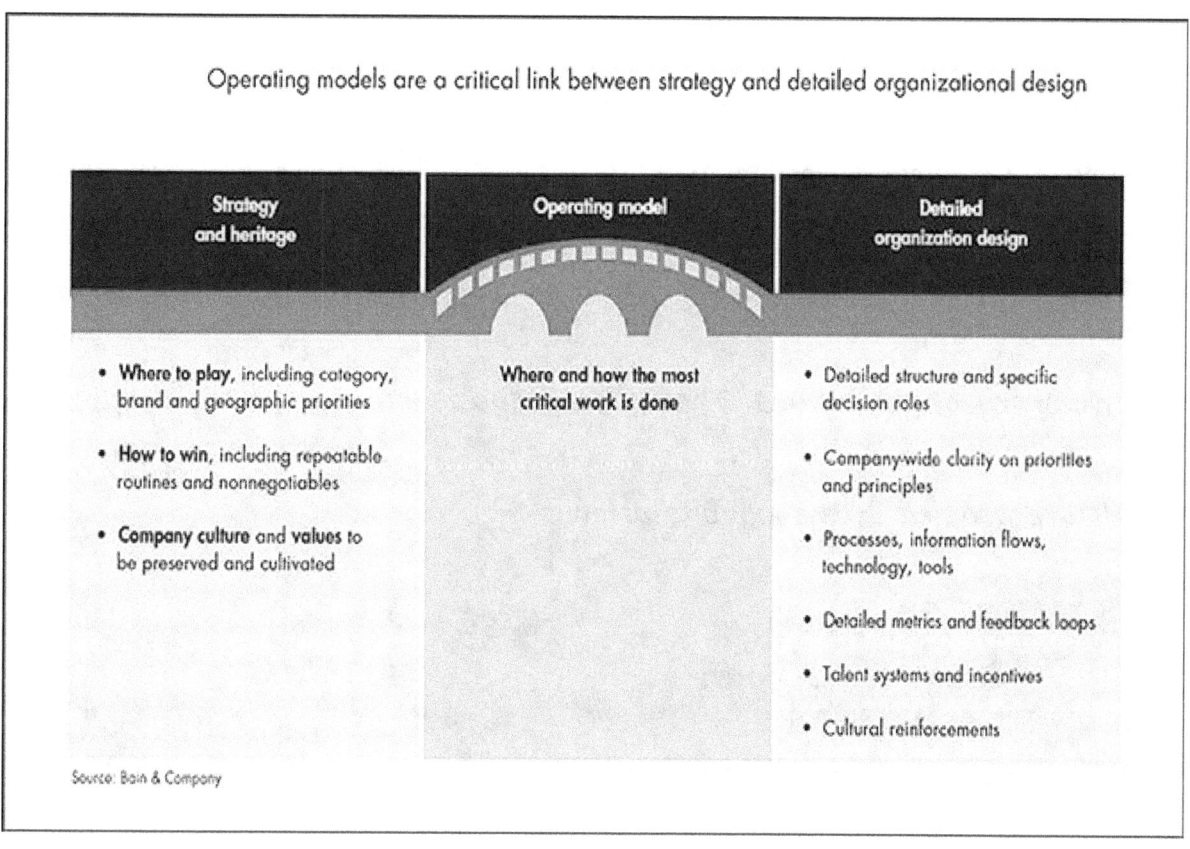

Operating models define the nature of interactions among the strategy, structure, people, processes and technology. Additionally, they also help realize the intended synergies that may arise in the interaction among these key organization elements. Thus, they help determine the rules of the game and need to be well conceptualized before the detailed organization design is laid down. Historically any discussion around the operating model invariably touches upon the perennial question of centralization versus decentralization. For ABC group this was no longer an either/or discussion so much as a question of balance. In arriving at the right delivery model construct, the team researched some of the key models being used by contemporary organizations. The salient aspects of each of these appraised models are profiled in the exhibits below:

Shared Service Model   Self-Service Model

Outsourcing Model   COE Model

Delivery Models of Optimization – An Overview

Shared Services Model	A collaborative model in which a subset of existing business functions are concentrated into a new, semi-autonomous unit that has a management structure designed to promote efficiency, value generation, cost savings, and improved services for internal customers of the organization. It provides a unique opportunity for organizations to leverage both, the economies of scale and depth of expertise
Self-Services Model	Self service as the name suggests, enables employees to complete much of their own transactional work, such as attendance and leave management, compensation structuring, etc on their own. This essentially unlocks the bandwith of some of the supporting functions, to focus on more their strategic aspects
Outsourcing Model	Under the outsourcing model the support activities identified to be carried out by a separate shared services organization, may actually be carried out by a third party outside of the overall organization. Focus on core capabilities, lowering operating costs, risk mitigation are some of the key triggers for outsourcing
COE/Hybrid Model	In a hybrid model, organizations may choose to deploy a combination of different delivery models such as shared services, outsourcing & self service. It mantains the flexibility for local, regional or national delivery, while setting standards and implementing best practices across the organization

Benchmark data[12] around these key operating model elements was leveraged by the TA & HR team at ABC. This helped guide their decisions in

---

[12] Winning Operating Models, by David Cooper, Sanjay Dhiri and James Root; Bain & Company

creating the right operating model and the organizational structure

construct as detailed in the following Exhibit :

Operating Model & Organization Structure Construct

Superstructure	ABC group's primary business units and how the P&L statement maps to them. This included role clarification of the envisioned operating model & its operational footprint
Governance Forum & Mgmt Cadence	To serve as Enablers for cross -group processes and interfaces to support strategic and operational decisions
Accountability	To Balance consistency with localized delivery of business units specific recruiting services
Behavioural Expectations	To establish how to work together appreciating the political, cultural & financial constraints in constructing the appropriate service delivery model
Outsourcing	Potential for outsourcing pieces of Talent Acquisition without loss of strategic & operational control
Talent Requirements	To make the operating model work. Type of Talent & skills required to support the hiring goals at ABC, Type of roles required & the hierarchial structure
Business Focus	To prioritize on functional areas that are key to the success of ABC' business units with appropriate resource allocation

It was important that the envisaged TA operating model & structure – the pattern of communication, authority, and work process flow relationships – at ABC were in sync with the business strategies. If the structure is compatible with strategy, then structure is an asset. If not – if, for example, a decentralized TA structure at ABC was not complementing its business expansion strategy – it was a weakness. A poor fit could cripple the best of the strategies because, in the end, every effective structure is a reflection of strategic intent and of the values & goals of the organization.

6.1.4   Process & Technology

In developing a business process, uniformity breeds quality and efficiency. Hammer and Champy defined a business process as "an organized group of related activities that together create a result of value to the customers." Under their definition, business processes are broader and more strategic in nature than business transactions. Business processes combine and coordinate transactions, cut across barriers of departments, time constraints, and bureaucracy; and are focused more on the needs of the customer and less on those of the processor — or his supervisor. But business processes have upper and lower boundaries. Built too large or trying to cover too much, processes become unmanageable behemoths that frustrate coordination and defy execution. Cut too fine, they lapse into transactions that add little value to the customer. As the process map, created by the ABC TA team, in the **Exhibit below** details, there are many separate transactions involved in each sub-process of the hiring life cycle. To evaluate the talent acquisition process in its entirety, it was considered practical to view its components on a granular level.

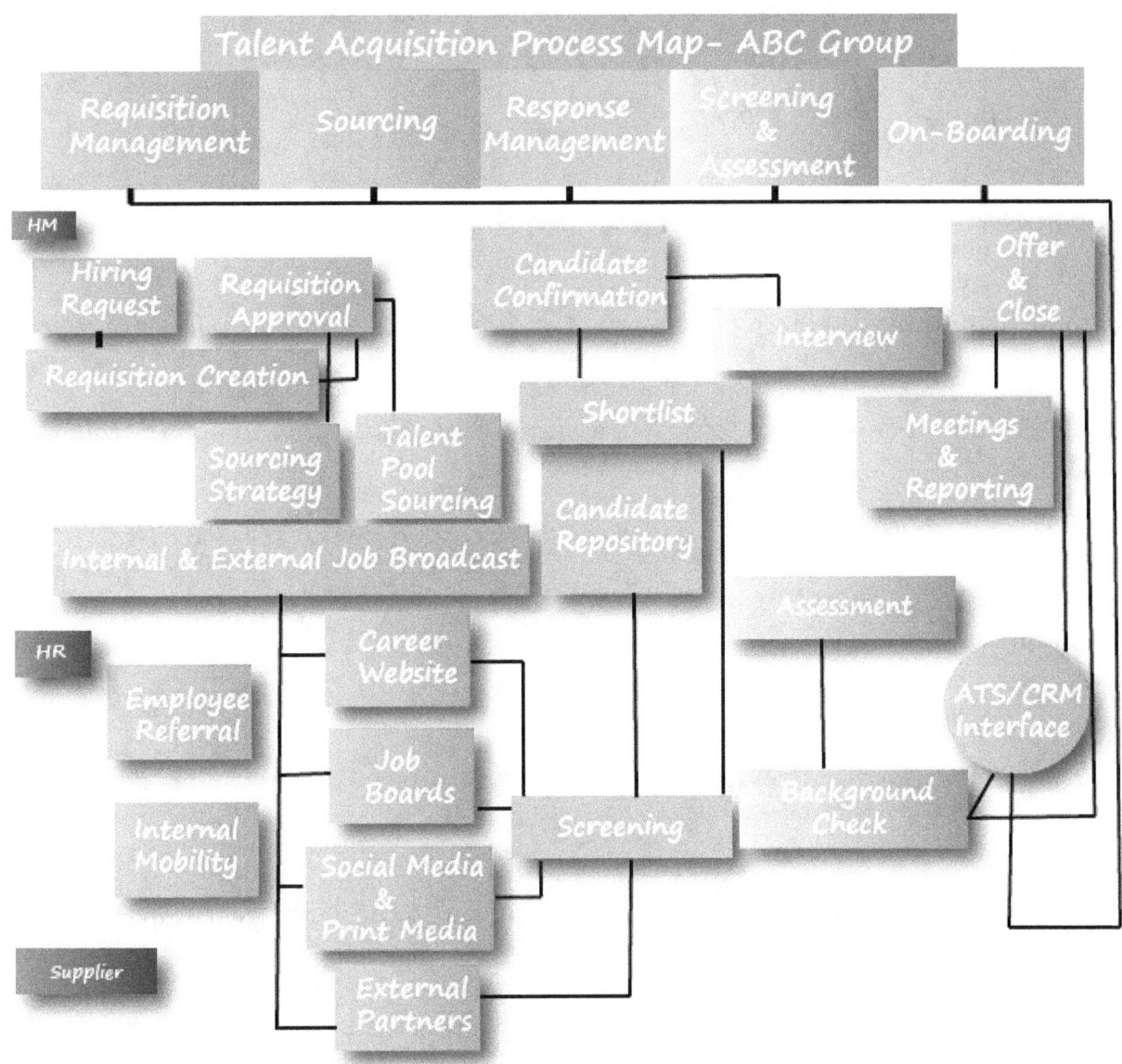

Managed as a disparate set of activities, work flow outputs from these process steps can have a detrimental impact on overall recruiting performance with no real value for the customers – the hiring managers and the talent prospects - who are more concerned with the quality and the timeliness of the outcome

A consistent process allows recruiters to improve efficiency and quality and establish tangible business outcomes. An end – to – end mapping exercise of the ABC recruitment process leveraging a number of **lean tools** detailed in the **sections below** was considered as a necessary next step in establishing baseline measures.

Voice of the Customer (VOC) and Voice of Business (VOB)

As one of the first steps, the ABC TA team conducted a voice of customer & voice of the business (VOB) data collection. This helped align what steps in the recruiting process cycle were critical to quality (CTQ) and were value – add versus non value – add. Key business unit heads and HR representatives who had all been involved in at least one recruiting process in the past were interviewed. Some representative questions to determine the customer needs, their relative importance and measurable CTQs (critical

to quality) are detailed below:

A	Which aspects of the recruiting process are important for you?
B	On a scale of 1-5, how important are these aspects for you?
C	How would you measure that the process is performing to your needs, and how would you know your expectations are not being met?

The results from this internal VOC were structured via a quality function

deployment (QFD), as shown below in the QFD | Exhibit

QFD 1

VOC \ CTQ	Importance	Total Cycle Time	Process Map & guidelines	Time to Schedule Interviews	No of Candidates Interviewed	No Of Candidates per Interview	Monthly Reporting	Offer Acceptance No Rework	New Hire in 1st Interview Round
Speedy Process	5	9		5	5	5		9	9
Clear Roles & Responsibilities	5	5	9	1			1		
Availability of the Hiring Manager	5	1		9					
Few Interviews Only		5			9	9			
Consistent Communication	3						9		
Fair & Competitive Offer	3							9	
Good Support from vendors	5	1							9
Total		105	45	75	70	70	32	72	90
		1	7	3	5	5	8	4	2

The most important CTQ's were summarized in a design scorecard

see Figure below . Using historically collected data a first baseline was

established that showed the performance of the customer requirements at the project start. This baseline information was leveraged by the ABC TA team to set the project goals.

Design Scorecard

CTQ	Unit	Specification			Continuous Data		Discrete Data
		Target	USL	LSL	Mean	Std.Dev	Success Rate
Total Cycle Time	Tage	70	75		120	15	
Time to Schedule Interviews	Tage	2	3		5	3	
Number of Candidates Interviewed	Anzahl	4	6	2	3.5	1.5	
Number of Candidates per Interview	Anzahl	1	2		2.3	1.1	
Offer Acceptance at First Time	%	95		80			55%
New Hire found in 1st Interview Round	%	95		80			35%

As a next step, the TA team conducted a functional analysis. In a process design, functions are high-level process steps. Developing functions enabled the team to define the necessary steps of the recruiting process without immediately having to think about solutions, detailed concepts or a detailed process design. In order to determine functions that would contribute the most in meeting the customer requirements the team used another QFD as illustrated in the QFDII Exhibit below

Function / CTQ	Importance	Requisition Creation	Sourcing	Response Management	Screening & Assessment	Offer Processing	Onboarding	Vendor Management	Technology Integration
Total Cycle Time	10	5	9	5	9	6	9	7	9
Process Map & Guidelines	5	2	8						
Time to Schedule Interviews	8	9					5		7
No of Candidates Interviewed	7	9	9	5	5				
No of Interviews per Candidate	7				9				
Monthly Reporting	3						2		
Offer Acceptance No Rework	7			9		9	9	6	
Total		195	193	188	188	123	199	112	146
		2	3	4	4	6	1	7	5

This set the tone for the detailed process development for the top prioritized functional areas. A representative **Design Element chart** for the prioritized functional areas is also profiled here:

Representative Design Elements

Design Element / Function	Recruiting Team Mix	Assessment Tools & Templates	ATS/CRM	Sourcing Channel Optimization
Onboarding	Specialist focus within recruiting team		Automated pre & post joining formalities	
Requisition Creation		Standardized JD/Requisition templates	Workflow automation for approval process	
Sourcing	Specialist sourcers & data miners in team	Sourcing Template Active/Passive candidates	Multiple channels search Functionality	Metrics driven channel selection to drive candidate flow
Screening & Assessment	Training in Interviewing Skills	Interview guidelines & feedback template	Pre-Hire Assessment & Interviewing tools	
Response Management		Preliminary screening & resume review	Resume parsing & indexing	Internal Talent Repository
Technology Integration	Performance Monitoring of recruiting team		Integration of disparate recruiting components	

SIPOC (Suppliers - Inputs - Processes -Output - Customers)

The suppliers, inputs, process, output, customers (SIPOC) diagram detailed below, essentially identifies at a high level the potential gaps (deficiencies) between what a process expects from its suppliers and what customers expect from the process, thus defining the scope of the process improvement activities. This process definition tool was leveraged to provide a high level overview of the Recruiting Life Cycle at ABC, importantly the In-Scope & Out of Scope activities. It additionally helped identify feedback and feed-forward loops between customers, suppliers and the process, jump starting the TA team to begin thinking in terms of cause and effect.

Suppliers	Input	Process	Output	Customer
External Search Partners Internal Hiring Team Employee Referrals Internal Talent Mobility	Resumes CV's Social Media profiles Performance Reviews	Requisition Management Sourcing Response Management Screening & Assessment Selection & On-Boarding	Selected Candidates Requisition Closure Quality of Hire	Hiring Manager Business Unit Heads HR Hiring Team SME Corporate Communications Marketing

Key benefits to the team are profiled in the Exhibit below

1	Enabled the ABC project team members to view the process in the same light
2	Visually defined the process at a high level & help define the scope of process improvements
3	As a first step in cause-and-effect thinking it contributed to understanding how the inputs, suppliers, process steps, and the outputs of the recruiting process cycle affect customer(s) needs
4	Helped identify gaps such as: * Inputs not needed but being recieved * Outputs that customer's don't want, but recieve anyway * Process steps that are completed, but add no value

Value Stream Mapping (VSM)

A lean process tool, value stream mapping is a fundamental tool to identify waste, reduce process cycle times, and implement process improvement. Some organizations treat the value stream map as the hallmark of their lean efforts. The power of value stream mapping lies in looking at the entire business process. More importantly, the mapping process not only includes defining the current state, but also includes defining the future state and the gaps between the two. With a clear picture of how the entire process should operate in the future, it becomes relatively easy to identify the interventions that will close the gap. The Value Stream Mapping exercise carried out by the ABC TA team, detailed in the Exhibit(s) below captured a current recruiting process cycle efficiency level of just over 18%. The low process efficiency implied that process leaks were occurring at various stages of its recruitment process cycle leading to value erosion at the end customer's end.

Current State – Recruitment Process Data

Activity	Process Time	Lead Time	% C&A	Tools	Stake Holders
Create Requisition	12 hrs	1 day	100%	Manual Semi Automated ATS	HM
Hiring Committee Review	3 hrs	2 days	70%	Email/Phone In-Person Meeting	HM, RT & HR
Sourcing Internal/External	8 days	5 days	85%	Email/Phone Internet/Intranet	RT, EP
Screening & Assessments	40 hrs	5 days	100%	Email/Phone SA ATS, Manual	RT, HR
HM Submissions & Interviews	7 days	20 days	95%	Email/Phone In-Person	HM, RT & HR
Selections & Offer Close	32 hrs	5 days	90%	Email/Phone SA ATS	HM, RT & HR
Offer Rollout Process	2 days	2 days	100%	Email/Phone SA ATS	HR, RT
Onboarding & Orientation	3 days	65 days	90%	SA ATS, Internet In – Person	HR, RT, HM BU Heads

HM: Hiring Manager RT: Recruitment Team
HR: Human Resource EP: External Partners BU: Business Unit Heads
% C & A: % complete & accurate

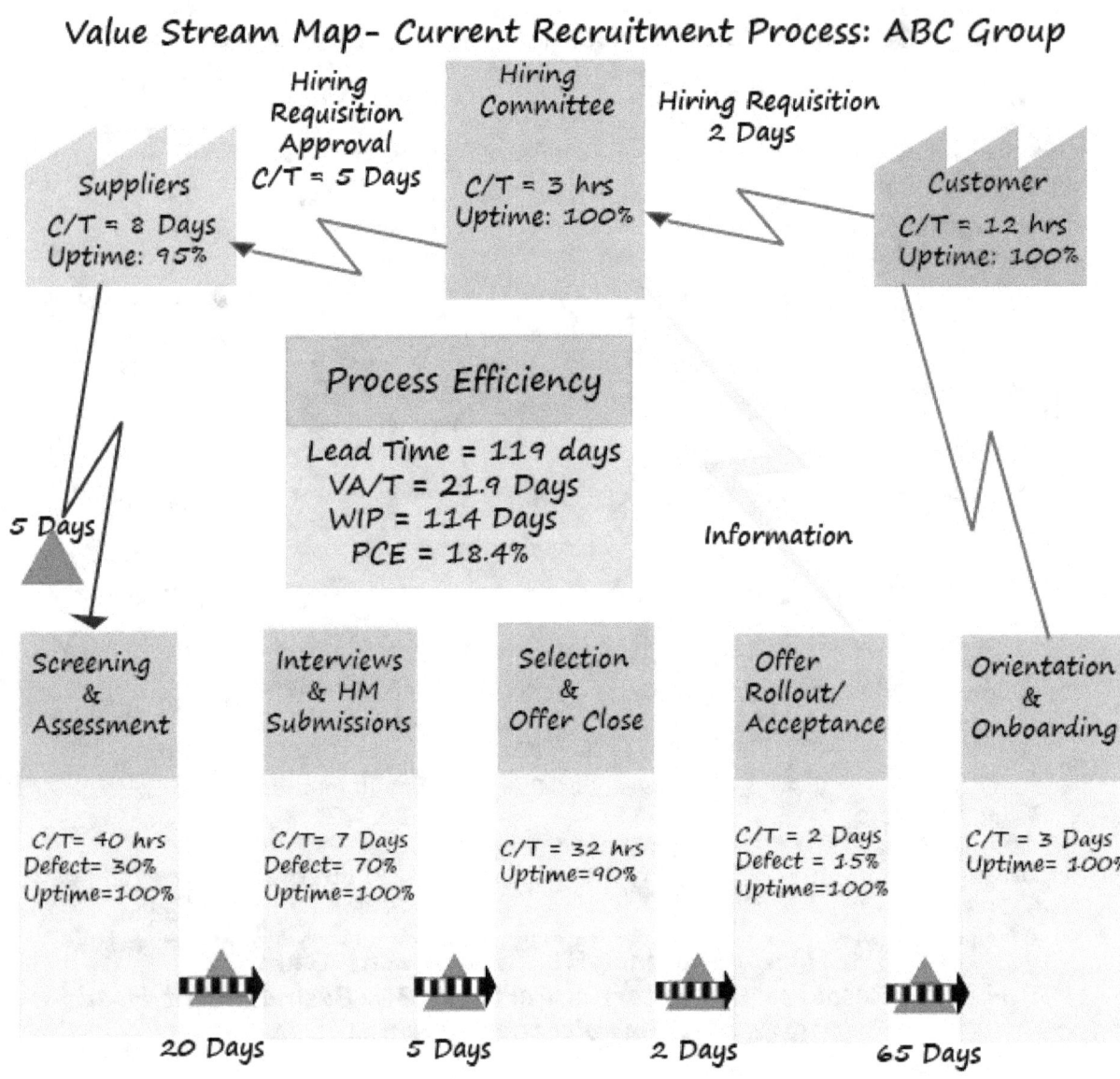

Value Stream Map- Current Recruitment Process: ABC Group

Hiring Requisition Approval C/T = 5 Days

Hiring Committee C/T = 3 hrs Uptime: 100%

Hiring Requisition 2 Days

Suppliers C/T = 8 Days Uptime: 95%

Customer C/T = 12 hrs Uptime: 100%

Process Efficiency

Lead Time = 119 days
VA/T = 21.9 Days
WIP = 114 Days
PCE = 18.4%

5 Days

Information

Screening & Assessment
C/T= 40 hrs
Defect= 30%
Uptime=100%

Interviews & HM Submissions
C/T= 7 Days
Defect= 70%
Uptime=100%

Selection & Offer Close
C/T = 32 hrs
Uptime=90%

Offer Rollout/ Acceptance
C/T = 2 Days
Defect = 15%
Uptime=100%

Orientation & Onboarding
C/T = 3 Days
Uptime= 100%

20 Days   5 Days   2 Days   65 Days

Process efficiency leaks [13]could occur as a result of lack of standardization In

process elements, talent acquisition tools and templates, missing service -

level agreements, activities between process units, within the HR function or

---

[13] Taleo Research White Paper – Hidden ROI of Talent Acquisition & Mobility, 2006

in interfaces with external service providers. Multiple touch points, integration and re-entry points in the process map were assessed for their contribution to the overall efficiency leakage. **Exhibit below** captures the process leaks at various stages of recruitment process cycle at ABC

TA Process Efficiency Leaks - ABC Group

Requisition Management	* Collaboration & decision difficult to manage * Routing requisitions for approval in hard copy or email is slow and not tracked * Documentation may be lost in inter-office paper shuffle
Sourcing	* Significant sourcing costs wasted due to lack of sourcing strategy, optimization effort on sourcing channel mix * Absence of governing policies on internal mobility & employee referral programs * Absence of SLA's with external sourcing partners
Response Management	* Lack of standardization on talent acquisition tools and templates. This included candidate screening forms, candidate communications, interview and evaluation forms, Job description templates, offer rollout guidelines
Screening & Assessment	* Absence of automated assessment tools * Absence of pre-hire assessment tools; HM Interview guide; intuitive hiring process * lack of recruiter training & development
Onboarding	* Need to standardize the onboarding process to optimize the onboarding experience & decrease time-to-full productivity

Talent Acquisition Process Map- ABC Group
Process Leaks

| Requisition Management | Sourcing | Response Management | Screening & Assessment | On-Boarding |

HM

Hiring Request

Requisition Approval

Requisition Creation

Sourcing
Significant costs wasted due to lack of a formal sourcing strategy
Lack of sourcing channel mix optimization

Offer & Close

Sourcing Strategy

Talent Pool Sourcing

Internal External Job Broadcast

Shortlist

Candidate Repository

Response Management

Lack of standardized TA process tools & templates

Requisition Management

Collaborations & decisions are difficult to manage

Requisition approval process lacks workflow automation

Absence of SLA's & Controls

HR

ATS/CRM Interface

Background Check

Screening

Supplier

External Partners

Absence of automated prescreeing tools
Absence of pre-hire assessment tools
Lack of Recruiter Training/Development Interventions

" Watch the little things. A small leak will sink a great ship." .... Benjamin Franklin

The wisdom behind Franklin's quote struck a ready chord with the TA & HR leaders at ABC as they went about the task of evaluating the process leaks in terms of staffing and unnecessary expenses and finally the opportunity presented to maximize customer value. The total economic value of process efficiency leaks was arrived at by combining the cost associated with inefficient application of internal staffing resources with the inefficient use of discretionary spending (e.g. external partners, print & online advertising). A cost measure of the often under –leveraged opportunity: internal mobility was also included. Awareness of the total costs of talent acquisition and mobility drove home the tangible benefits possible through process improvements at ABC. The following Exhibit from a White Paper by Taleo Research succinctly underscores this substantive value proposition to the ABC stakeholders.

Summary of Value Wasted

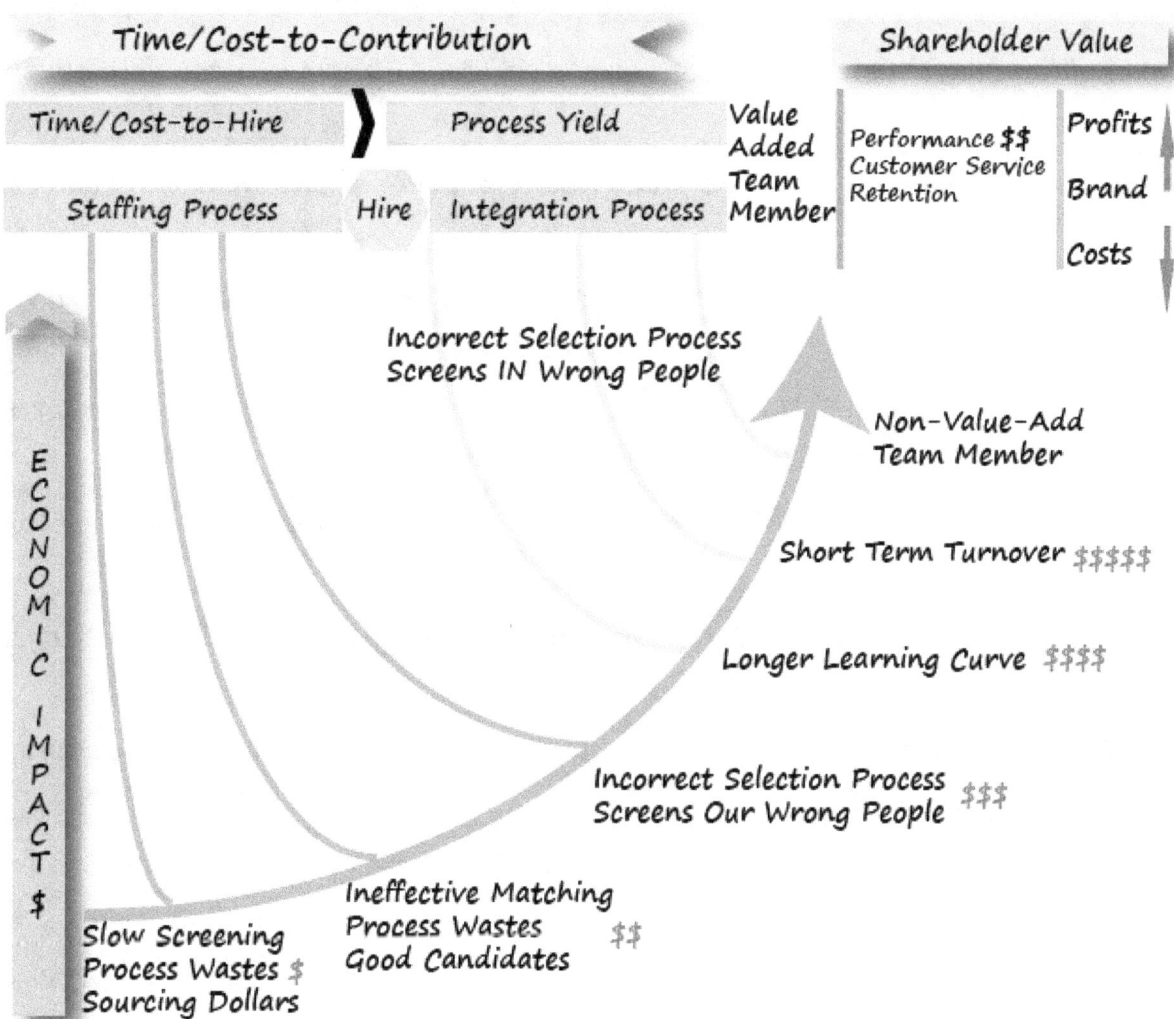

While the efforts to optimize the recruitment process were on, key stakeholder constituents at ABC were also focusing their attention on the supporting technology solutions that would provide them with the required domain expertise and address the unique challenges and strategies involved in recruiting top talent. There was broad consensus within the team that to deliver real value, recruitment operations must be supported by best-of-breed ATS/ CRM solution that encompass the entire pre-hire life cycle including candidate acquisition, requisition management, job postings, search capabilities,, interview management, communications, and performance reporting. Beyond the alignment of technology and process, the team looked at criteria specific to the technology itself as detailed in the exhibit below

Search Functionality	Sourcing capabilities from within the ATS on multiple sourcing channels e.g. job boards, social media, internet sourcing on candidates and keywords & boolean search strings
Adoption & Usage	Would the system be used by all stakeholders? Would data be captured comprehensively for all reporting purposes?
Integration	Would the system have capabilities to "talk" to other technology components affected by the talent acquisition, Can CRM,onboarding, payroll, assessment & interviewing components be integrated seamlessly?
System Administration	Do we need to create a designated, single point--of contact for adressing technical & functional issues? Who would have the ability to accomplish minor configuration changes?
Candidate Experience	Would the system foster a positive candidate experience through career site branding, online employee referral programs, assessments, social media, mobile capabilities, vendor management, candidate self-service applications?
Cloud Vs IT	Will the system be delivered on our IT Infrastructure or can be based on a cloud server through third party resources?

The exercise provided valuable insights on the efficacy of its current processes and supporting technologies to maximize efficiency and productivity and the desired process & technology state.

6.1.5 Metrics & Measurement

Metrics, Analytics & indices are the language of performance monitoring and as the cliché goes: "You can't improve what you can't measure.", and by not measuring, the recruiting organization misses an important opportunity to learn from its own processes – what it is doing well and how it is adding value to the organization? – Lack of a metrics driven recruiting culture at ABC and the excessive reliance on historical metrics was considered a major inhibitor in focusing limited resources on tools & strategies that have a significant business impact. After spending, time, money and resources on optimizing Talent Acquisition, it was important to demonstrate the business case. The following steps were considered key to establishing an appropriate metrics driven performance process:

Alignment to ABC' corporate objectives: Measuring against relevant business needs and that the results hold value for business leaders

Establishing Key Performance Indicators: Both business facing KPI'sthat directly impact bottom-line and operational metrics that apply to the Talent Acquisition function

Baseline Performance: Leveraging current & historical data to appraise performance relative to the KPI's

Constructing a Talent Acquisition Scorecard or dashboard

The final step in creating a **Talent Scorecard** was seen as a way to elevate the visibility and importance of the Talent Acquisition function within ABC and demonstrate a strong commitment to select and onboard the best talent relevant to its business needs.

The Key stakeholders also deliberated on the common pitfalls – **refer Exhibit below** – to avoid in creating the right numbers and measures to include in the Talent Scorecard.

Measuring the Wrong Things	Companies frequently measure activities, time and cost because it is easy to get these data. It's mush harder to measure quality, results & value ~ data that counts
Focusing on the Trivial Many vs the Vital few	The art in measurement is to focus on a core set of indcators that are truly meaningful. It is best to focus on 8-9 meaningful, consequential measures
Moving Beyond Summary Data	Average figures can mask significant variations. It is important to "slice" the data to look for meaningful patterns and trends
It's what you do with Data that Matters	Metrics are only valuable if they result in better & informed decisions

Starting with the Right Questions

The process of finding the right measures for the Talent Scorecard at ABC

was not easy. There was an initial tendency to go too narrow, too quickly

but subsequently the approach piloted around getting the bigger picture

right and not identify specific metrics too early in the process. The big picture was centric around the market focus of ABC group and the strategic initiatives planned to support its business goals. The important next step was to concentrate on the right questions to ask for the Talent Acquisition practice area and its alignment with the planned strategic initiatives. In formalizing a matrix of measures, the following list of questions was gleaned from research, best practices[14] and ABC group's historical data points.

---

[14] Adapted from "Talent Metrics that Matter", Human Capital Institute, USA

Representative " Library of Measures"

What is the relative strength of our employer brand among leading candidates?

Are we attracting diverse Candidates?

What percentage of first-choice candidates accept our offer?

What % of candidates do hiring managers deem unqualified?

Do our assessments correlate with future performance & success?

What is the average time-to-hire?

How many strategic jobs are unfilled?

Is there a backlog of candidates for hard-to-fill positions?

What % of employees participate in employee referral programs?

How many applications are recieved per type of open position?

What % of total hires come from employee referrals?

How long does it take employees to become "job proficient"?

What recruiting sources provide the best employees & future high potentials?

What % of new hires remain in the company 12-18 months later?

The Strategic Filter

With these questions in mind, the next step for the team was to winnow the list based on the organization business context and priorities. For instance, an organization may not have a turnover issue; or because it has a younger workforce, retirement eligibility and the need to maintain a deep bench strength may not be of concern. These factors can accordingly be omitted from the Talent Scorecard. For ABC group attracting top talent for key strategic roles supported by a flexible recruitment delivery model was a strategic imperative to fuel its business growth plans and create competitive advantage. The next filter applied was to array the organization strategy and initiatives, and alignment of the proposed measures to them. The draft scorecard thus prepared was shared with key business stakeholders for their inputs and buy-in.

A representative outline of this scorecard construct is presented in the

Figure below

Building the TA Scorecard - A Representative Outline

Strategic Insights/Questions	Strategic Alignment/ Rating	Data Access Rating	Outcome Measures
% of new Employees with 12-18 months tenure	5	5	Candidate Experience, Engagement Index
% of Hires from Employee Referrals	4	5	Engagement Index
Type, expertise of people dedicated to TA	5	4	Quality of Slate, Recruiters Cost Ratio
% of 1st Choice Candidates who accept the offer	5	5	Talent Brand Index
Average Time-to-Hire	5	5	Cost of Vacancy, Time to Proficiency
Recruiting Sources providing best candidates/HIPOs	5	4	Sourcing Channel Efficiency
% of Hard -to-Fill Positions	5	4	Recruiting Competition, Candidate Availability
Time to Job proficiency	5	5	Quality of Hire
No of applicants per position	3	5	Employment Brand
% of Strategic jobs unfulfilled	5	5	Bottom-Line Impact, EVP

Applying this strategic filter paved the way for creation of a Talent Acquisition Scorecard of key metrics & measures that could be recorded, monitored and tracked. This would ensure ABC is better aware of its most significant talent acquisition practices and accordingly guide its efforts & actions in support of attracting, engaging & acquiring critical organization talent. The final Talent Scorecard construct is profiled towards the end, in the Best Practices section of this e-book

Benchmarking for Success

Integration of Talent Acquisition Solutions
with
Talent Management Systems

As the foregoing sections reveal, the selection and implementation of talent acquisition solutions and their integration with various talent management systems plays a crucial role in the ability to turn these strategies into vehicles for performance and growth.

The TA picture which emerged through the lens of the **strategy framework** was an environment drawn between the forward-thinking and the status quo with visible gaps in the <u>functionality and vitality</u> of its talent acquisition practices. Organizations today are a blend of both characteristics, but understanding "**Where are we today?**" and "**What do we know?**" provided valuable insights on ABC's ability to compete for talent in the future and helped clarify its talent acquisition agenda. What is presented in the **Exhibit(s) below** is a comparison of **market centric, result driven** versus **passive approaches** that were in practice in each of these areas at ABC group. The **functionality dimension** – the processes, systems and tools that allow a company to put the right people with the right skills in the right place at the right time - shows that ABC had its work cut out In the areas of sourcing, workforce planning, assessment processes, employment branding and technology integration. Similarly the **Vitality dimension** – manifested by the passion for talent acquisition among key constituents: top management, line management, HR & TA team and the talent pool itself —

shows that despite high commitment all the segments in ABC group are

weak on accountability, and the top team is weak on engagement as well.

Since a company's talent acquisition process is only as strong as its weakest

link, and vitality falls apart without mutual accountability, ABC clearly had

a lot of work to do.

Sourcing Tactics & Strategies

Results Driven

Employee Referral Program	Networking with Professional Organizations	Campus Recruiting
Searching Online Databases	Direct Sourcing & Headhunting	External TA Partners

Passive

Dependency on Job Board Postings Post & Pray Strategy	Waiting for Candidates to find Job Postings or Adverts	Less leveraging of social media tools, internal mobility & talent mapping

Recruiting Operations Tactics & Strategies

Results Driven

Optimizing Recruiter Time for recruiting not administration

Improving Hiring Manager Engagement

Balancing Best-in-Class processes with local recruiting needs

Vendor Performance Management

Online Assessments & Support

Passive

Recruiter Job Postings, Interview set-up/ coordination

Hiring Skewed through External Partners

Low reliance on Pre-Hire Assessment Tools

Talent Acquisition System & Solutions

Results Driven

Optimizing Current Technology

Balancing Technology capabilities, new areas for improvement & process changes

Adding Selection Data & Tools into Application Tracking Systems (ATS)

Passive

Adherence to Old Paradigms such as posting & filtering Vs social networking & active candidate outreach

Lack of integration allowing disparate systems to remain unconnected

Recruitment Strategy

Results Driven

Workforce Planning to provide predictive, precision forecasting

Talent Pipeline Model Supply Chain Principles

Talent Acquisition An Improvement Initiative, not an overhead process

Focus on EVP Employer Value Proposition

Passive

Focus on reactive recruiting/ empty postion firefighting

Workforce Planning Straight Line, Constant Growth Rate Based

Lack of Metrics & Measurement Systems

Lack of TA culture for external talent marketplace and internal talent needs

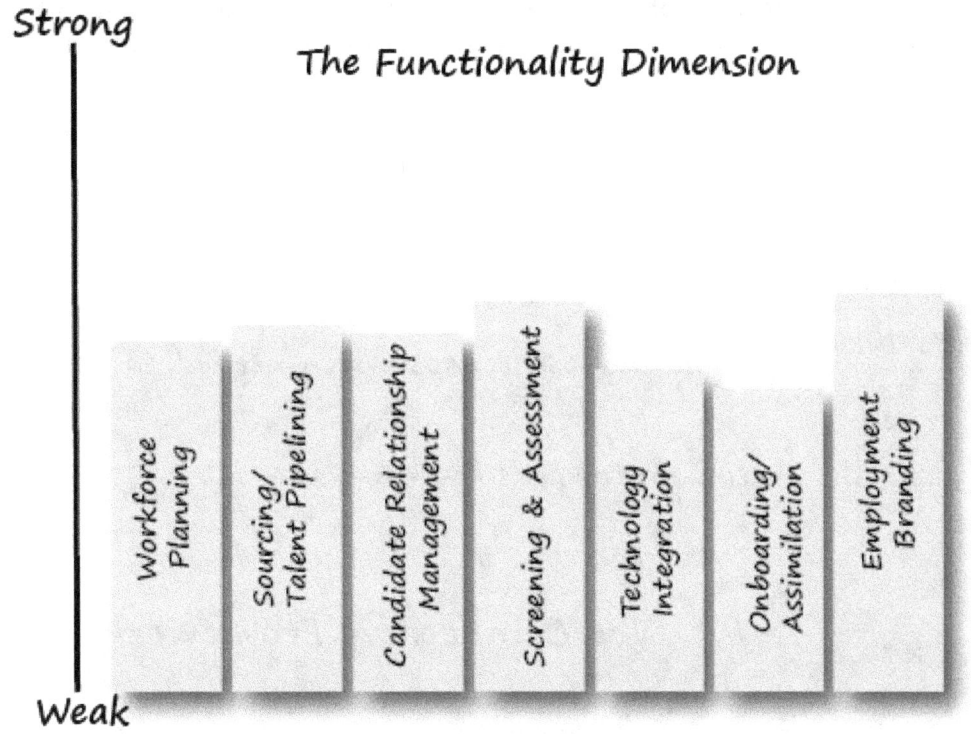

The Functionality Dimension

Strong

Weak

Workforce Planning

Sourcing/ Talent Pipelining

Candidate Relationship Management

Screening & Assessment

Technology Integration

Onboarding/ Assimilation

Employment Branding

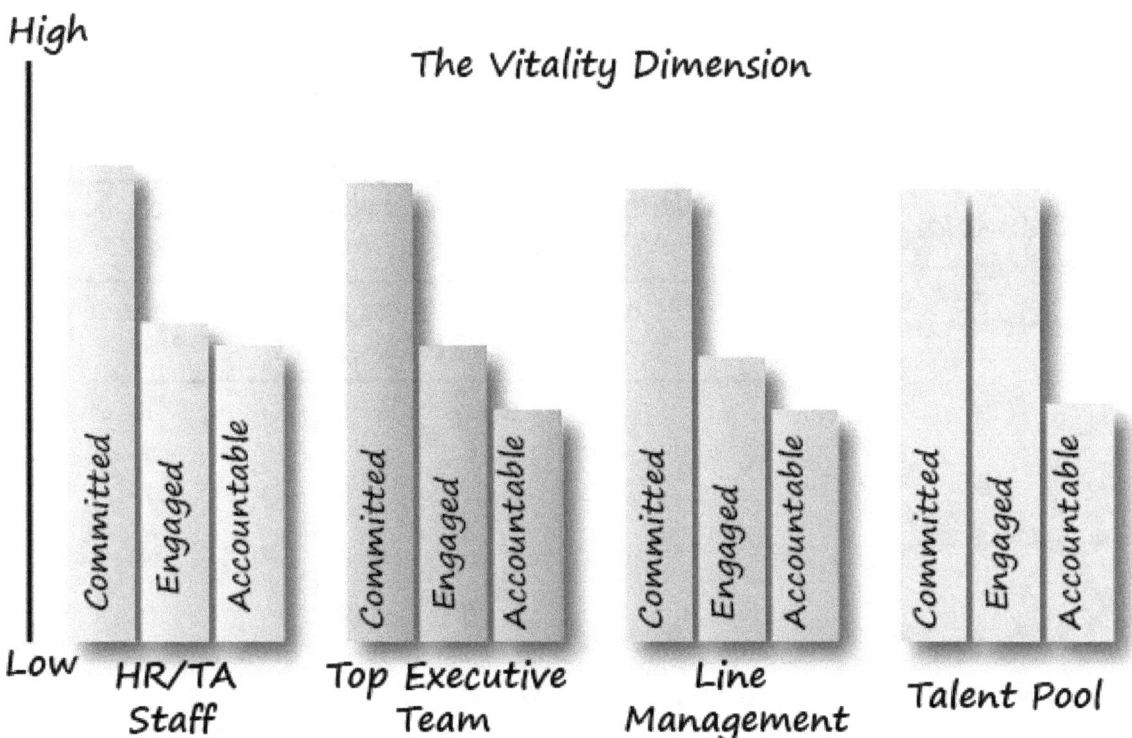

The Vitality Dimension

High

Low

Committed — Engaged — Accountable — HR/TA Staff

Committed — Engaged — Accountable — Top Executive Team

Committed — Engaged — Accountable — Line Management

Committed — Engaged — Accountable — Talent Pool

117

This composite picture of ABC' current talent acquisition practices and performance were subsequently mapped to a **Competitive Framework** based on a research study by the Aberdeen Group. The Exhibit(s) below highlight the visible gaps which needed to be bridged to move along the continuum towards best-in-class.

The Competitive Framework

Process	Job roles deemed most critical to organization's success have been identified
Organization	Standardization across all aspects of recruiting
Knowledge	Core competencies are defined at the start of hiring process Screening is strategic and does not require a single error
Technology	Talent Acquisition technology currently in use ATS/ Assessments/Internal Job Portal
Performance	Metrics to measure success have been agreed upon by key stakeholders

Source: Aberdeen Group, September, 2013

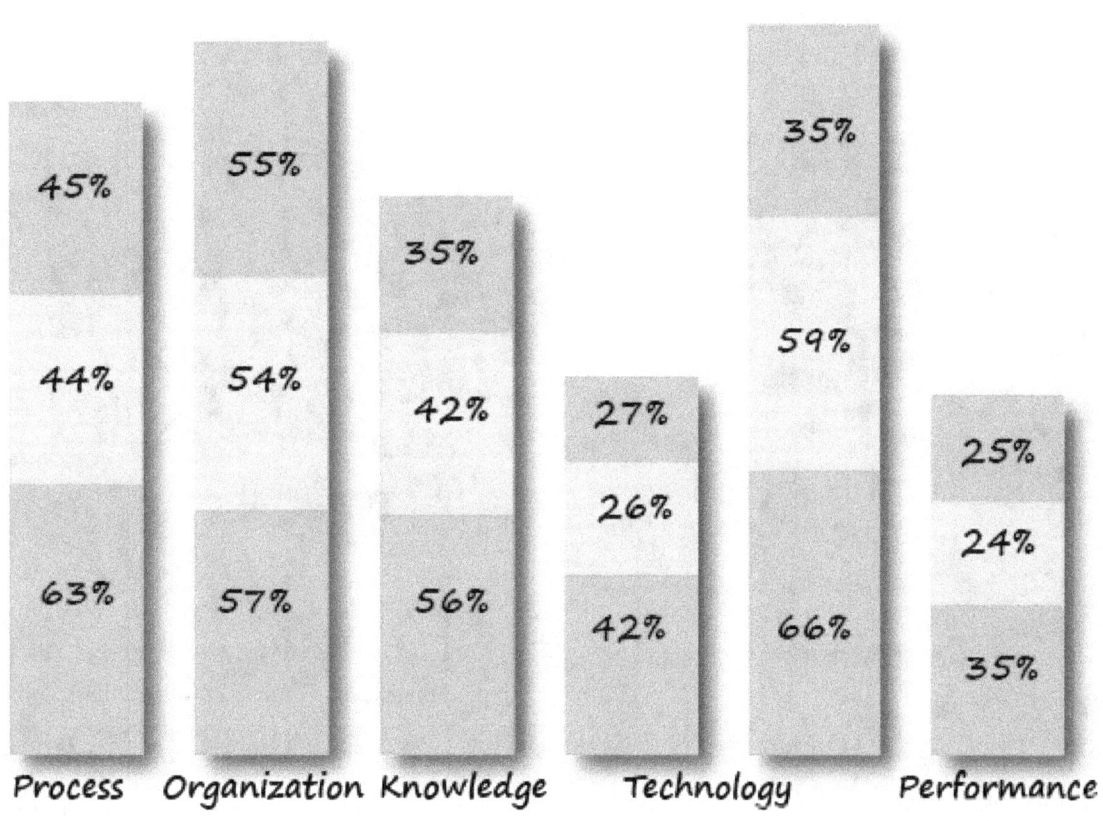

Legend:
- ABC Group
- Average
- Best-in-Class

	Process	Organization	Knowledge	Technology	Performance
ABC Group	45%	55%	35%	35%	25%
Average	44%	54%	42%	59%	24%
Best-in-Class	63%	57%	56%	66%	35%

Technology also shows 27% and 26% in the overlapping section, with 42% below.

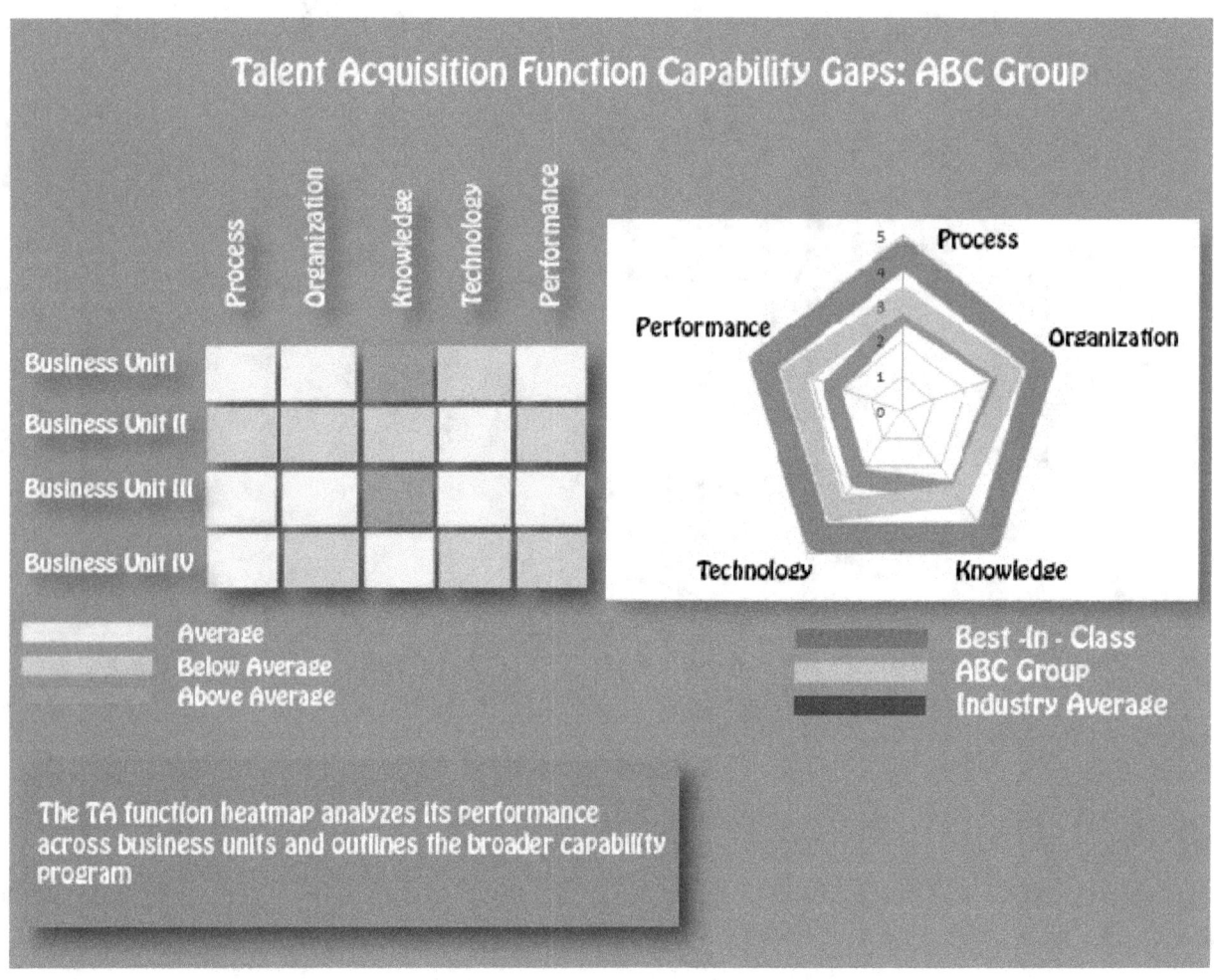

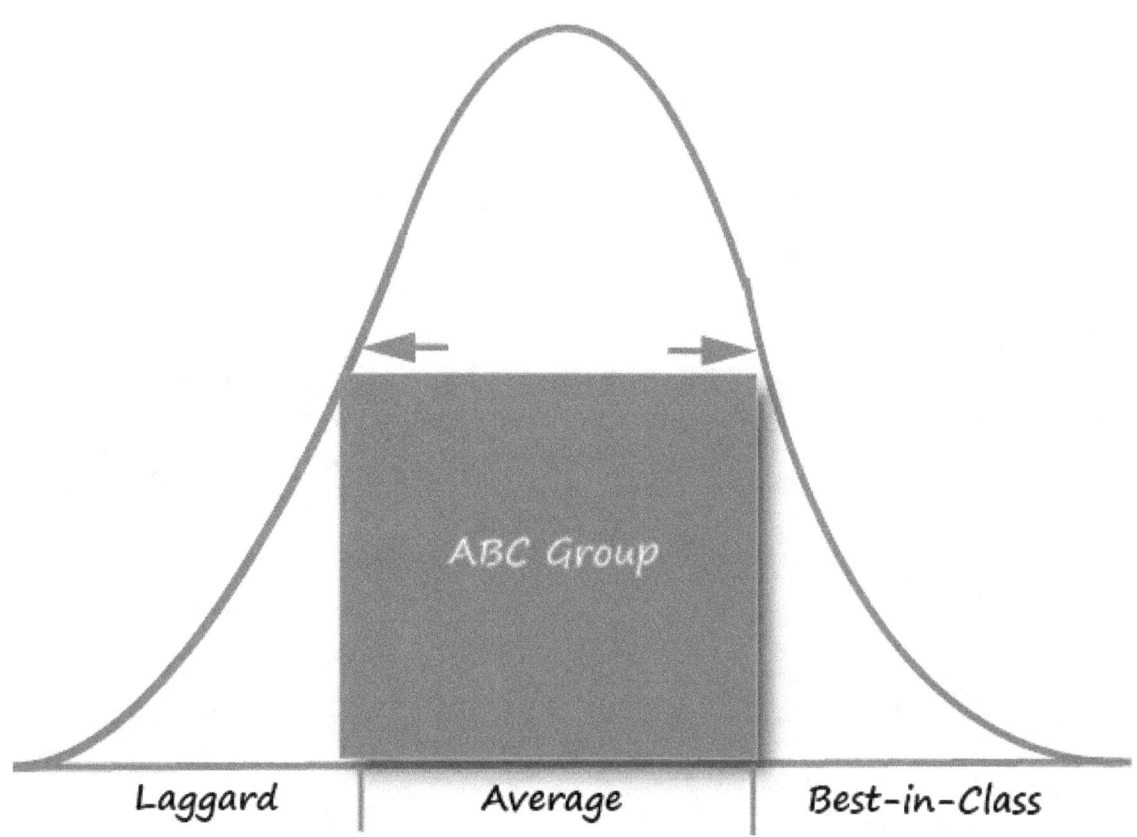

the good news: there was a genuine intent to innovate and move towards best-in-class recruiting practices at ABC group

The Key challenges and expectations that emerged as a consequence of ABC

group's assessment of its current Talent Operations are detailed in the

Exhibit below

Challenges & Expectations

Alignment of the TA function with organization goals & mandates

Leadership Imperative: Fostering committment, engagement and accountability among key constituents

Need for efficient and responsive recruitment processes as pressure to acquire top talent intensifies. Technology to be a key enabler for efficiency

Effective utilization of existing resources, resource productivity, hiring cost and talent sourcing channel mix

Re-orient focus from Quantity of Hire and "More is Better" philosophy to Quality of Hire

Find the best candidates "in" the market, not just "those on" the market

Globalizing the Talent Acquisition Strategy to facilitate finding, attracting & on-boarding diverse talent within new geographies

In summary the task was to re-engineer a dispersed Talent Acquisition function and navigate the shift from a necessary business process to a business-critical partner

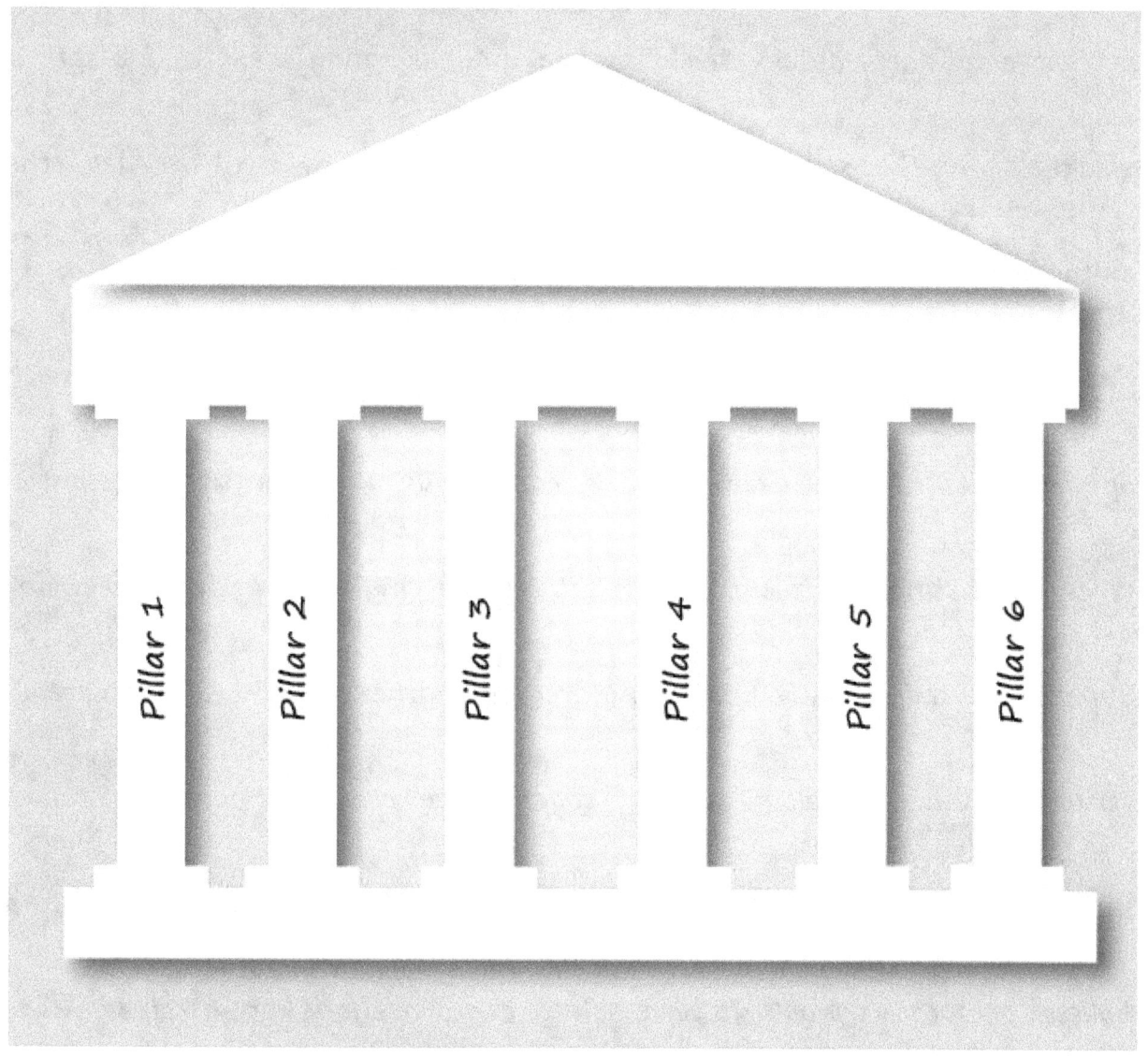

Brand, Strategy, Structure, Process and Technology represented an

effective framework for assessing ABC' talent operations at a high level. For

example, what often appear to be technology shortcomings are actually caused by inadequate organization structure. Likewise, the inability to attract candidates as effectively as one may like may seem to indicate a weakness in the strategy or overall structure – when, in fact, the employment brand may be the root of the problem.

The issues that challenged ABC' talent operations presented it with opportunities for improvement, and continuous improvement is essential when competing for talent. The reality is, no single strength, problem or opportunity falls exclusively into one area or another. ABC' brand, strategy, structure and technology worked together to create a complete talent picture, and so their workings were highly interconnected. Applying a holistic perspective wouldn't have solved the challenge, but it helped make sure that the organization was asking questions that considered the complete workings of its talent operations.

The foregoing sections highlighted the tactical and dispersed character of the Talent Acquisition function at ABC and that much work needed to be done in terms of improving the recruiting process efficiency, laying down &

standardization of key metrics to quantify the ROI, creation of shared

knowledge repository within the function, bridging skill & competency gaps

within the recruitment teams across group companies, and overall

promoting a clear line of sight on how Talent Acquisition should be evolved

as a strategic function to qualify successful business outcomes. In line with

the overall approach of aligning recruiting with business, the Talent

Acquisition strategy construct was designed specifically to complement and

build on the corporate success tenets at ABC which included:

Corporate Success Tenets at ABC Group

Operational Excellence	Market Leadership	Professionalism Ethics & Brand Image
Fiduciary Responsibility to our Clients		
Continuous Innovation in all Businesses, Products and Processes		

This corporate success template was then reduced to a 'Recruitment Charter' centric around the following goals:

Recruitment Charter
ABC Group

Build a Staffing function around supply chain principles with a profit centre orientation

Be Considered Strategic & an extension of the business units

Inculcate a customer centric approach in servicing the hiring managers business talent needs

Demonstrate value by quantifying the ROI of the TA function

Improve delivery by creating innovative efficiencies within the function

Identify, attract & hire top talent for existing and new business markets, geographies

The Recruiting charter paved the way for the creation of a **Recruitment Centre of Excellence (COE)** envisioned as the lynchpin of a business facing talent acquisition strategy at ABC. **The key considerations**, that went into the creation of the COE included:

Flexible Delivery Model	The COE would accomodate the key advantages of central & decentralized models. It would drive standardization around best practices across the organization, yet also enable business -specific adaptation and customization based on differing needs of each of ABC' business units. While offering greater process efficiency and clear structure, it could be architected with fungible resources and delivery models that could shift to sudden changes of demand or business strategies
Standardizing Processes & Key Metrics	The present recruiting processes & key performance indicators had a siloed outlook in various business units and were failing to provide business leaders with an accurate view of talent acquisition deliverables The COE would serve as a hub to standardize processes around job requisitions, interviews & assessment methodologies, service level agreements (SLA's), employer branding services, metrics & analytics and on-boarding best practices
Continuous Improvement	By organizing key operational elements in a COE, ABC would be assured that this entity would seek to organize itself around pockets of knowledge & expertise and will stay abreast of key industry trends and innovative practices in talent acquisition. Laying down of apt hiring metrics to measure the efficiency and effectiveness of the recruiting process was considered integral to the recruitment approach

Competitive Advantage	Talent Acquisition should be viewed as a mechanism to provide the organization with competitive advantage by increasing its business capabilities through recruiting more of the right talent
Strategic Workforce Planning	With the uncertainty in business environment becoming the new normal, need was felt to transition to a workforce planning model which could accurately forecast talent demand right down to the individual job and minimize the mismatch costs. The COE, it was envisaged would serve as an objective, authoritative, evidene-based source of workforce analysis & planning expertise and build deep understanding of talent supply & demand centric to ABC group's business areas
Strategic Intervention in New Hiring Markets	In line with its global aspirations ABC group was increasing its footprint outside India to the Middle East and West Africa geographies. Sustainable success in these new markets would hinge around its ability to find, attract, and retain diverse talent within a completely new landscape. This would require a deep understanding of the cultural job preferences of the target talent community and the COE was expected to provide the requisite recruiting expertise

The COE delivery model was in effect a distributed process arrangement where the recruitment process was delivered using a combination of different delivery models. The same is illustrated below:

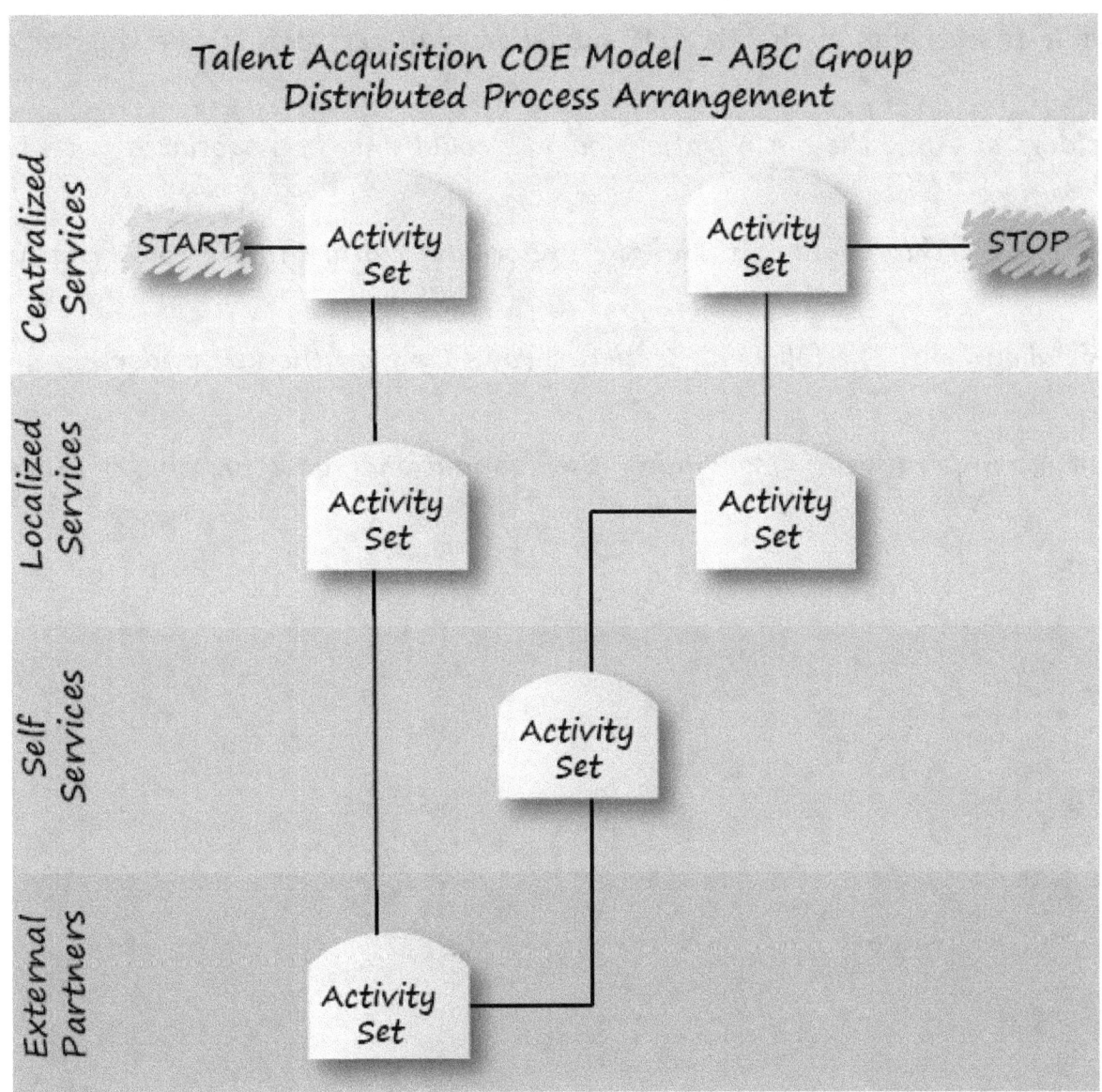

While the benefits of the TA COE model were understood by the key stake-holders at ABC, the optimization journey could only be negotiated with the right leadership alignment and the underlying culture fabric to strengthen this alignment. The following section throws light on the key leadership and culture imperatives in solidifying the foundational base for the envisaged COE.

8 The Leadership and Culture Imperative at ABC Group

Creating an optimized TA COE with a sustainable outlook required extraordinary commitment from the leadership coterie across the various business units within ABC including key HR & TA functionaries.

The leadership imperatives expected included:

A	Assessing the potential benefits of the optimization opportunity against the associated risks
B	Effectively conceptualizing the plan to leverage on the opportunities provided by optimization
C	Managing complex stakeholder relationships while executing the plan to leverage the optimization opportunity
D	Managing the change process so as to institutionalize the changes required
E	Enabling a culture of optimization within the affected functional area and other key affected constituents

Realizing the above outcomes required the ABC leadership team to demonstrate behavioral competencies different from their usual set of expected behaviors. This implied an adjustment to the existing leadership framework. The following leadership competencies displayed in the **exhibit below** were considered integral to the overall competency framework for leaders involved in the talent acquisition optimization effort

Change Leadership	Creating a compelling business case for change & identifying critical success factors and potential obstacles to change
Relationship Leadership	Influencing & gaining buy-in to the desired agenda from multiple quarters. Building coalition of support and overcoming barriers
Execution Leadership	Demonstrating ability to convert strategies into effective & systematic implementation plans. Ensuring flawless execution focusing on reducing costs & time, and benchmarking against the best
Business Results Leadership	Exhibiting drive & energy towards achieving goals & results; mantaining high perfromance standards. Displaying 'entrepreneurial effort' through ownership and co-creation

Source: Adapted from KPMG in India Analysis

The Leadership imperatives apart, the talent acquisition capability maximization effort required tapping into the collective mindset of the people - the **organization culture**. This Collective mindset – that is, shared ways of thinking or shared cognitive patterns- has two powerful outcomes. It defines the way people behave, and it also determines what information people will accept, interpret accurately, and adopt as useful knowledge. One powerful definition of culture is therefore, the shared ways of thinking that determine how people both inside and outside the organization collectively behave and what information they collectively accept and use[15]. An organization whose culture cannot accurately perceive, think, and interpret its environment and effectively translate those perceptions & interpretations into employee behaviors will have great difficulty in staying in business[16]. Such shared assumptions are the most fundamental and non-malleable aspect of creating an optimized organization[17]. The following

---

[15] Source: Developing a Human Resource Strategy, Wayne Brockbank, University of Michigan
[16] ibid

dimensions of culture **Exhibited below** were considered important to be strengthened towards creating an optimized mindset by the Leadership at ABC group

[17] Jossey Bass, Organization Culture and Leadership, Edgar.H.Schein, 3rd Edition

Leadership at ABC had a very critical role to play in building the right mindset in engineering the optimization effort. The re-orientation to the required leadership behavioral competencies was largely instrumental in providing the traction for this change process.

9 Building the Talent Acquisition COE Structure

The primary objective of the recommended Recruitment Centre of Excellence **(COE) model** within ABC Group was to provide centralized delivery on core strategy and operational elements, while ensuring localized delivery of business specific recruiting services. It housed an infrastructure capable of delivering high volume tactical services, centralized recruiting knowledge base and expertise to deliver best practices and standardized recruitment services. The COE had a scalable, flexible character with focus in three specialized areas – please see Exhibit(s) below

Sourcing – Focus on leveraging innovative technologies, savvy market analysis and targeted outreach strategies to attract the best available talent with the sourcing team responsible for building the talent pipeline

Sourcing

| Direct Recruitment | Talent Pipeline Creation | Database Mining & Resume Screen |
| Postings & Ad Placement | Social Media & Diversity Strategies | Market Research & Analytics |

Operations – Focus on the efficiency and effectiveness of the hiring process with the operations team responsible and accountable for the logistics and administrative components of the talent acquisition process

Operations

Background Checks	Budget & Cost Management	Vendor Management
Metrics & Measurement	Standardization of Recruitment Process	Offer Process & Onboarding
Interview Scheduling & Coordination	Online Assessment & Support	

Recruiting – Focus on managing the candidate and hiring manager relationships to ensure right fitments and positive experience for all stakeholders and promoting a strong ABC employment brand

Recruiting

Employer Branding	Workforce Planning	Global Standards
Internal Mobility	Campus Hiring & Internships	Interviews & Assessment Standards
Requisition Management	Pipeline Management	Hiring Manager Relationship

The specialized focus areas in the **COE** allowed the Talent Acquisition team at ABC to work as specialist consultants in areas of policy creation, process optimization and strategy formulation. It was suggested that businesses do not lose sight of the tactical recruiting services whilst building confidence in the new delivery model. The scope of services provided thus varied between the various group companies and their individual needs. A key factor which helped shape and influence the scope of services provided was the underlying technology supporting the COE model. Implementation of a Global Applicant Tracking System (ATS) was a step in this direction. By providing the customers (all ABC group companies) with one recruiting service touch point for all the tactical processes, the **COE** would enable a consistent, personalized service across multiple communication channels. The **COE,** envisaged as the main access link to clients seeking recruiting information electronically, made it imperative that the team members be **customer-focused** advisors who provide advice and guidance on recruiting-related matters across the service chain, with the more complex enquires being passed through to Consultants and Project Managers to address. The **COE** was proposed to be governed by Service Level Agreements (SLA's) to measure and monitor the overall effectiveness and efficiency of the service rendered, cascading down into internal process measures and individual team member objectives.

The **Exhibit below** captures a representative "scope of services" outline

drawn up for the recruiting COE at ABC

Representative Scope of Services
TA COE – ABC Group

Centralized Recruiting Functions	Localized Business Unit Recruiting Functions
Workforce Planning	BU Specific Resourcing
Sourcing Strategy & Channel mix Optimization	Recruitment Process Execution
Managing Candidate Audiences	Demand Forecasting
Metrics Generation & Monitoring	Candidate Generation/ Sourcing
Employment Branding	BU Process Standards
Technology Optimization	Line Managers Coaching
Process Standards and Practices	BU Specific Reporting & Analysis
Content Marketing	
Research & Benchmarking	
Campus Relations	
External Partners Management	
Stakeholder Management	

9.1 The Key Recruiting Transformation Stages – ABC Group

Research shows that Recruiting professionals can spend up to 40% of their time on administrative tasks like data tracking, interview scheduling and documentation related to offer generation. The introduction of a **COE** model at ABC provided an opportunity to release Recruiters and Recruiting Managers from process related activities, allowing them to focus their skills on the realization of departmental business plans and strategic issues within the organization. Improved processes and new technology integration helped administer the efficiency savings and service delivery desired through a focused operation. Over and above this, the transformation exercise enabled a new 'business focus' dimension to the career of the Talent Acquisition team members leading to increased personal achievement and job satisfaction.

Transforming the delivery of recruiting services is a complex multi-faceted program of work which impacts all parts of the organization. Transformation programs, which may include related activities such as hiring manager and candidate satisfaction, are typically delivered in a number of phases over an extended period of time. This period is determined by the complexity and scale of the transformation, its priority within an overall recruitment program and the organization's attitude to risk. Research* indicates that there are typically three main staging areas in an organization recruiting transformation journey: **Strategic, Technology and Tactical** leading to the creation of the **Talent Acquisition Center of Excellence (COE) model.** . The Exhibit below captures this phase-wise journey of the ABC group highlighting the salient aspects of each phase

Recruiting Transformation Stages - ABC Group

Phase I - Laying down of ground map, process flows, communication channels, Rationalization of procedures - 2-3 months

Phase II - Technology Interface, Installation of Global ATS, Improved accountability, reporting & metrics tracking - 3-5 months

Phase III - Tactical phase; CoE fully operational; cost & efficiency gains 10-12 months

Building Human Capital	Best-in-Class Talent Sourcing & Acquisition TACoE
Ensuring a Ready Talent Supply	Best-in-Class Innovations Preparing for the Next Generation of Talent at ABC Group

9.1.1   Phase I

The first step of work is the Strategic phase, which usually occurs in early stages of the program and was covered in detail in the "Strategic Framework" section above. Within this stage a strategic vision is set with change management initiatives in place to embark on the new model with new processes fully embedded within the organization, capable of providing professional recruiting services to all business units. A strategic plan is set to focus on efficiency gains which are made through process improvements, automation of manual tasks, innovation through new technology and rationalization of procedures. The **Value Stream Mapping (VSM) of the current recruiting process** – detailed in the foregoing section- revealed areas of low quality and helped identify "waste" to be targeted for elimination. The exercise allowed the ABC recruitment team to produce a future state VSM that was free of the identified waste and non-value-added activities. Visually, as depicted below, it provided a map for the

recruitment team at ABC to follow.

Types of Wastes in Lean – "Muda"

7 Types of Waste	Recruitment Process Flow
Waiting	Escalations/Approvals, waiting for offers, feedback
Inventory	Offers to be processed resumes to be reviewed
Defects	Incorrect data, requisitions not updated
Over Processing	Updating ATS/ TAS
Transportation	Multiple Interviews, Shipping Offer Letters
Over Production	Work -in -Process Inventory, Processing prior to need
Motion	Tracking down paperwork, Walking to and from printer, fax, filing cabinets

If **VSM** represented the roadmap for ABC' Lean Recruitment journey, then

5S, a lean principle, provided the necessary fuel. To initiate the required

culture shift 5S was introduced in Phase –I to serve as a foundation for all

recruitment   process   improvements.   These   5   essential   principles

refer Exhibit below for operating in a Lean environment helped ensure

process consistency

5 S Principles in Lean

SORT
Separation of necessary activities from unnecessary
Identifying Waste

Set In Order
Organize activities according to their order of importance
An enabler of Efficiency

Shine
Structure work area for sorted and set-in-order activities
Workplace Hygiene

Standardize
Ensure Sort, Set-in-Order & Shine steps are consistently
followed
Reducing Process Variations

Sustain
Maintain & Improve, sort, set-in-order, shine
& standardize steps
Ensuring Lean Efforts are continuous

Following the VSM and 5S, the TA team focused on the _Kaizen opportunities.._ Early efforts in the phase 1 to standardize processes and improve quality are captured in the Exhibit below

Value Stream Mapping – Kaizen Opportunities

A Requisition Approval Process aided by workflow automation with appropriate auto-notifiers & escalation points

ATS/CRM capabilities integrated with sourcing & assessment tools, job boards & external partners

Standardizing initial candidate phone -screening; Skype or Video Interviews

Creating a compliant process for documenting search strings

Creating a Interview Reference guide for hiring managers

Creating a check list for Offer Compliance

Documenting the Employee Referral Process

Internal Mobility, redeployment process for internal hires

Matrix of Actionable & Predictive Hiring Metrics

Introducing a Kanban for Offer Letters

Implementation roadmaps – including timelines and milestones-were developed for each process improvement opportunity, and prioritized based on the business impact.

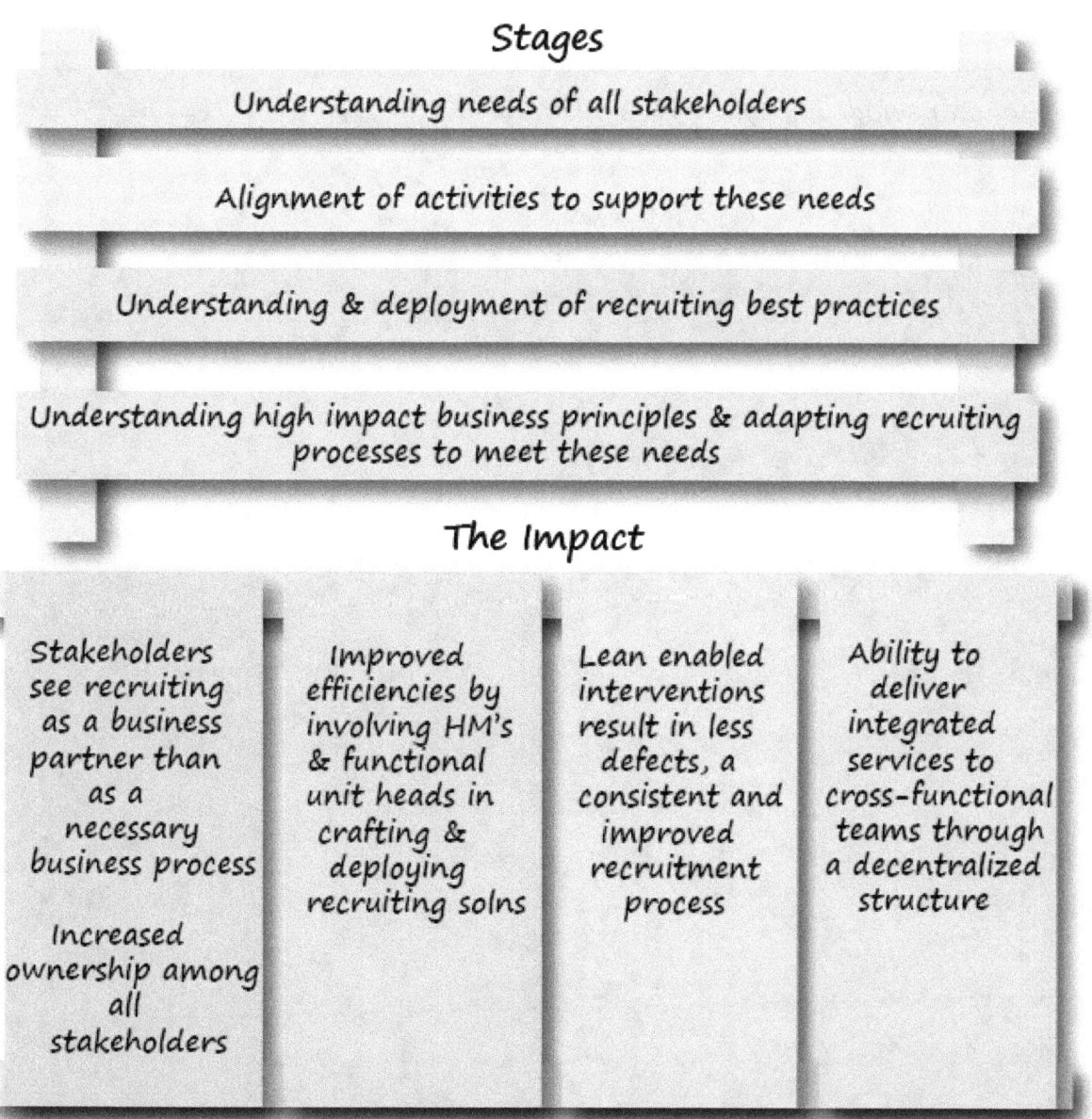

9.1.2 Phase II

The second step of the transformation was the Technology phase (Introduction of a Global TAS) and the rollout of the new reporting and metrics framework. The projected implementation period was spread over a five month period

Stages

Understanding impact of technology on the entire recruiting life cycle

Selection & Deployment of technology to support these needs

Alignment of Technology to complex recruiting scenarios

Establishment of metrics scorecard within technology systems to populate an easy-to-understand performance dashboard

The Impact

Leveraging technology for delivery of highly efficient tactical & strategic recruiting

Improved process efficiency in delivery of services

Improved Accountability

Improved reporting & metrics tracking

9.1.3 Phase III

The third step of the transformation phase involved full operationalization of the COE recruiting model, a culmination of around twelve months of phase wise reengineering efforts. The phase was characterized by realization of cost savings and efficiency gains as a consequence of the re-designed processes, reduced headcount and technology integration

Stages

Full Implementation of re-designed processes and enabling technology encompassing all process stages of the recruiting life cycle

Optimization of staffing headcount and restructuring of the recruiting team around specialist business areas and functions

The Impact

Delivery of highly efficient tactical services leveraging technology

An effective service delivery model demonstrating efficieny in streamlining services

Centralized sourcing function that is efficient & effective

Interaction with group companies and feedback driven by processes, policies & SLA's

An operational framework in place to drive adaptation of enterprise-wide best practices

Efficiency & Effectiveness norms become the driver to achieve operational excellence

153

9.1.4   The Final Phase

The final step in the Optimization phase involved maintaining process improvements through continuous process control. It entailed making sure the recruiting process improvements continued to add value to the business units and the organization as a whole. A risk analysis for the new process was conducted using the failure mode and effects analysis (FMEA) approach. An extract of this **FMEA** is shown in the **figure** below:

FMEA
Failure Mode and Effects Analysis

Process Step	Potential Failure Mode	Potential Failure Effects	SEV	Potential Causes	OCC	RPN
Conduct Interviews & present Shortlist	Quality & Quantity of Shortlist	No Fitment case	5	Sourcing Channel Mix not appropriate	4	20
				Location/Comp issues	3	15
				Role Specs/JD not defined properly	5	25
Brief Interviewers	Recruiter Interviewing Skills	Interviewers make wrong hiring decisions	7	Lack of Recruiter Training Inputs	5	35
		Undesirable candidate experience	7	Hiring Process of recruiting staff	5	35

SEV = Severity   OCC = Occurence Rate   RPN = Risk Priority Number

The goal was to make sure the right people and resources are in the right place at the right time to fulfill business needs. This is the stage when the Talent Acquisition function starts adding real value to the business by partnering and proactively bringing a business partner perspective to business decisions. Recruiting and HR strategies are well aligned with the business and returning people investment.

The Impact

Demonstration of Quantifiable Value to the Business

Recruiting Strategies fully aligned to Business Needs

Provision of Subject Matter Expertise & Expert Advisory Services through the COE

Recruiting Integrates as a Business/Strategic Partner

Benchmarking a norm to accelerate Learning and provide Stimulus to Change

Flexible Delivery Model responsive to Changing Business Needs

It is pertinent to mention that in order to optimize on the timelines, factor in the interdependency aspect of the various recruiting process steps, and enable desired cost efficiencies, the phase-wise transformation effort was run concurrently rather than as disjoint events.

10 Talent Acquisition at ABC Group – The New Perspective

The recruitment transformation effort helped ABC group embrace, "Talent Acquisition" as a mainstream business function, which impacts all areas in the Talent Management value chain, from building a strategic employment brand, through sourcing and recruiting, all the way to on-boarding top talent. The complexion and character of the transformed function was stronger, with branding, talent pipelining, strong assessment practices at its core, and a cohesive integration with the business.

Findings based on an _Industry Leading Talent Acquisition framework made famous by Bersin By Deloitte_ **refer Exhibit below**

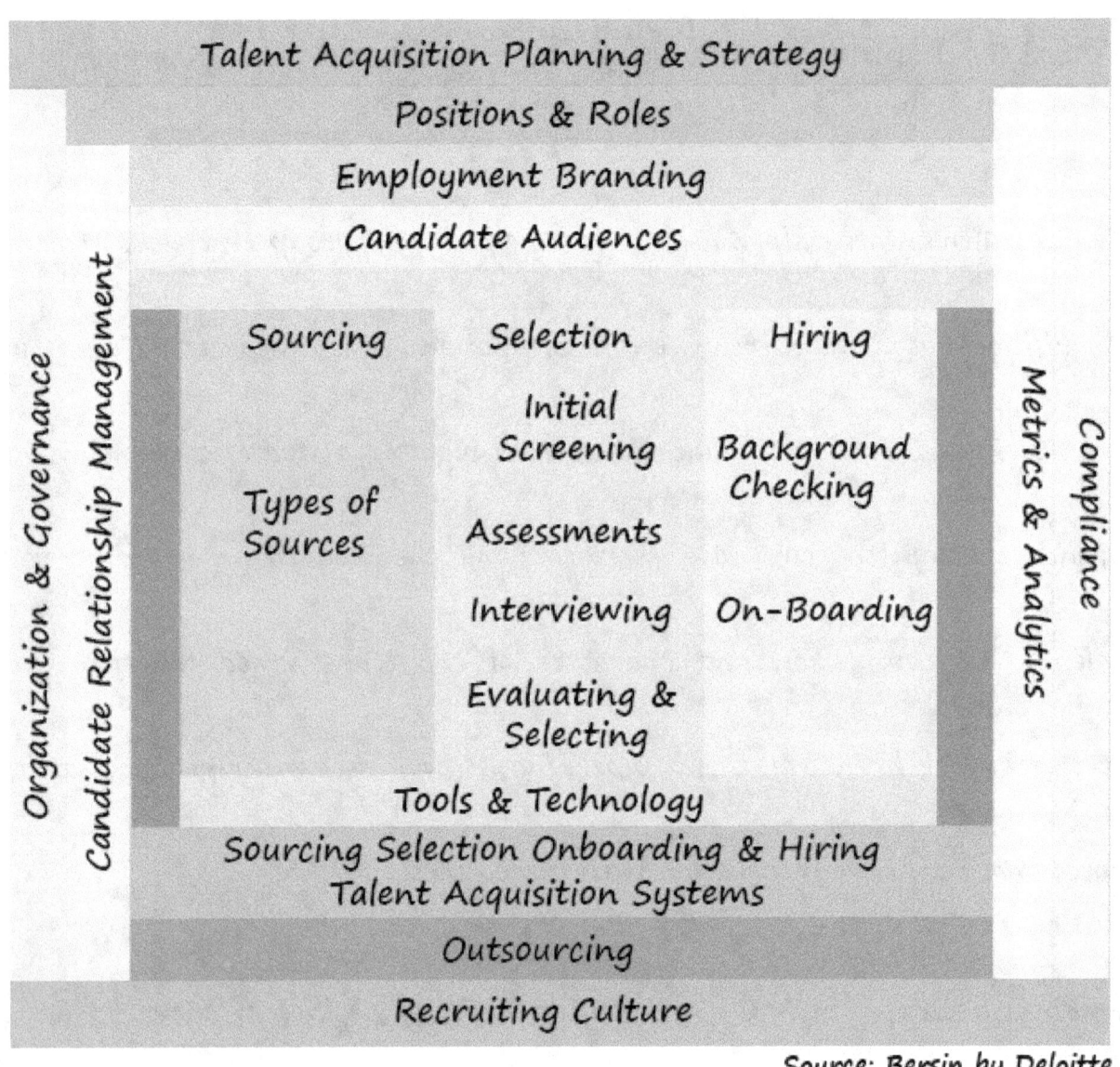

Source: Bersin by Deloitte

underscored the fact that while recruitment is an essential element of talent acquisition, organizations need to bring a broad end-to-end focus to enable a composite view of their talent operations encompassing the process areas as profiled in the Exhibit below

Planning & Strategizing

Workforce Segmentation

Delineating Candidate Audiences

Candidate Relationship Management

Creating, Validating & Maintaining an Employment Brand

Defining Metrics & Conducting Analysis

Creating an Organizational Recruiting Culture

The Bersin Talent Acquisition Framework, in particular, is meant to help organizations understand talent acquisition in today's business climate and how it fits into the broader context of talent management. Even if an organization's talent practices, processes and supporting technical systems are robust and up to date, talent management will fail without a deep-seated commitment from senior executives. Passion must start at the top and infuse the corporate culture, otherwise talent acquisition processes can easily deteriorate into bureaucratic routines. The Bersin framework essentially highlights this fundamental precept, which formed the core of the new TA perspective at ABC and successfully helped optimize the function. This success in great measure lay in the group's ability to marry **functionality**, rigorous talent acquisition processes to support strategic and cultural objectives, and **vitality**, emotional commitment of its key stakeholders.

Mapping Functionality and Vitality at ABC Group

The functionality and vitality of ABC' re-engineered Talent Acquisition processes were pivotal to its ability to attract, engage and onboard best-in-class talent. The figure(s) below illustrate the visible improvements in both the functionality and vitality dimensions as a consequence of the optimization effort. Readers may refer **section 4.1** towards a realistic appraise

The Functionality Dimension – Reengineered TA Function

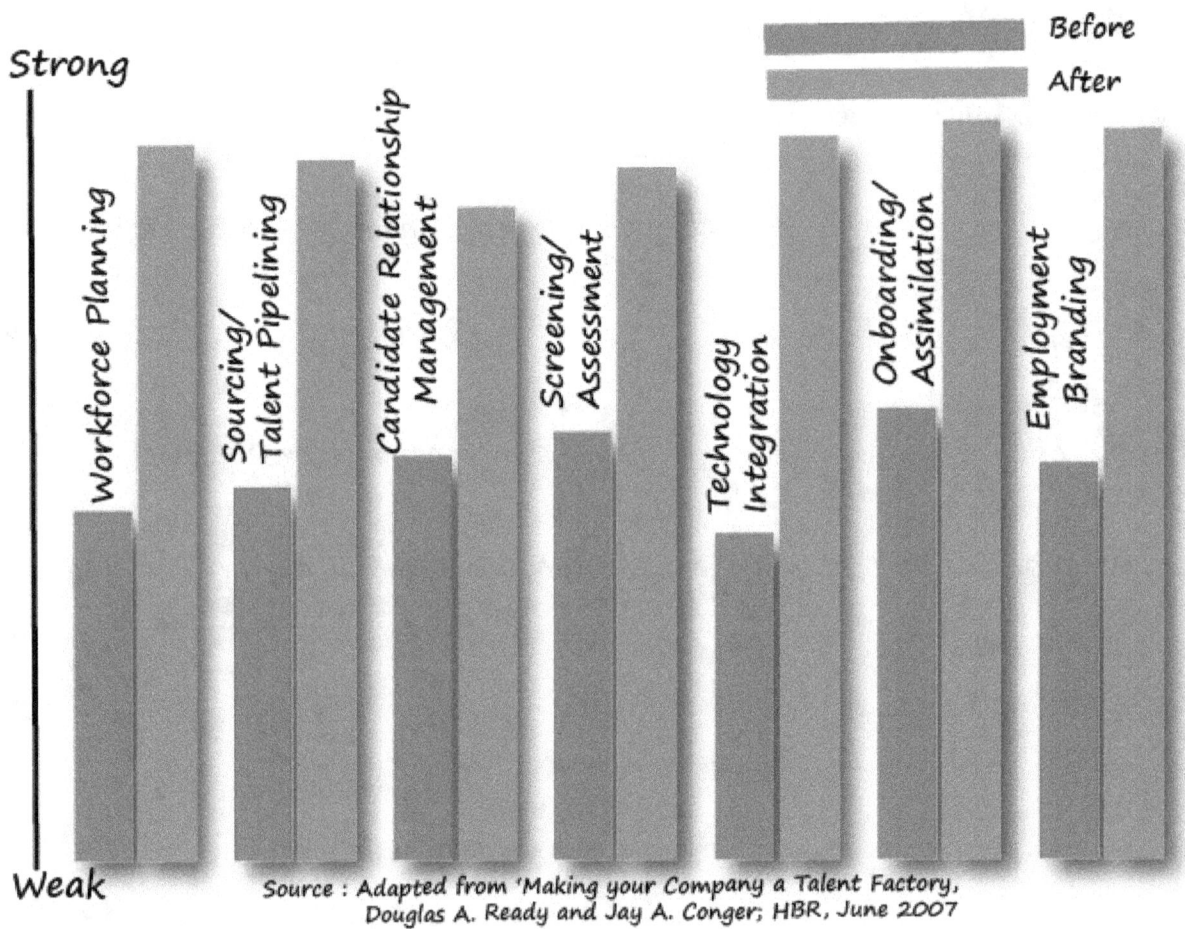

Source : Adapted from 'Making your Company a Talent Factory,
Douglas A. Ready and Jay A. Conger; HBR, June 2007

The Vitality Dimension - Reengineered TA Function

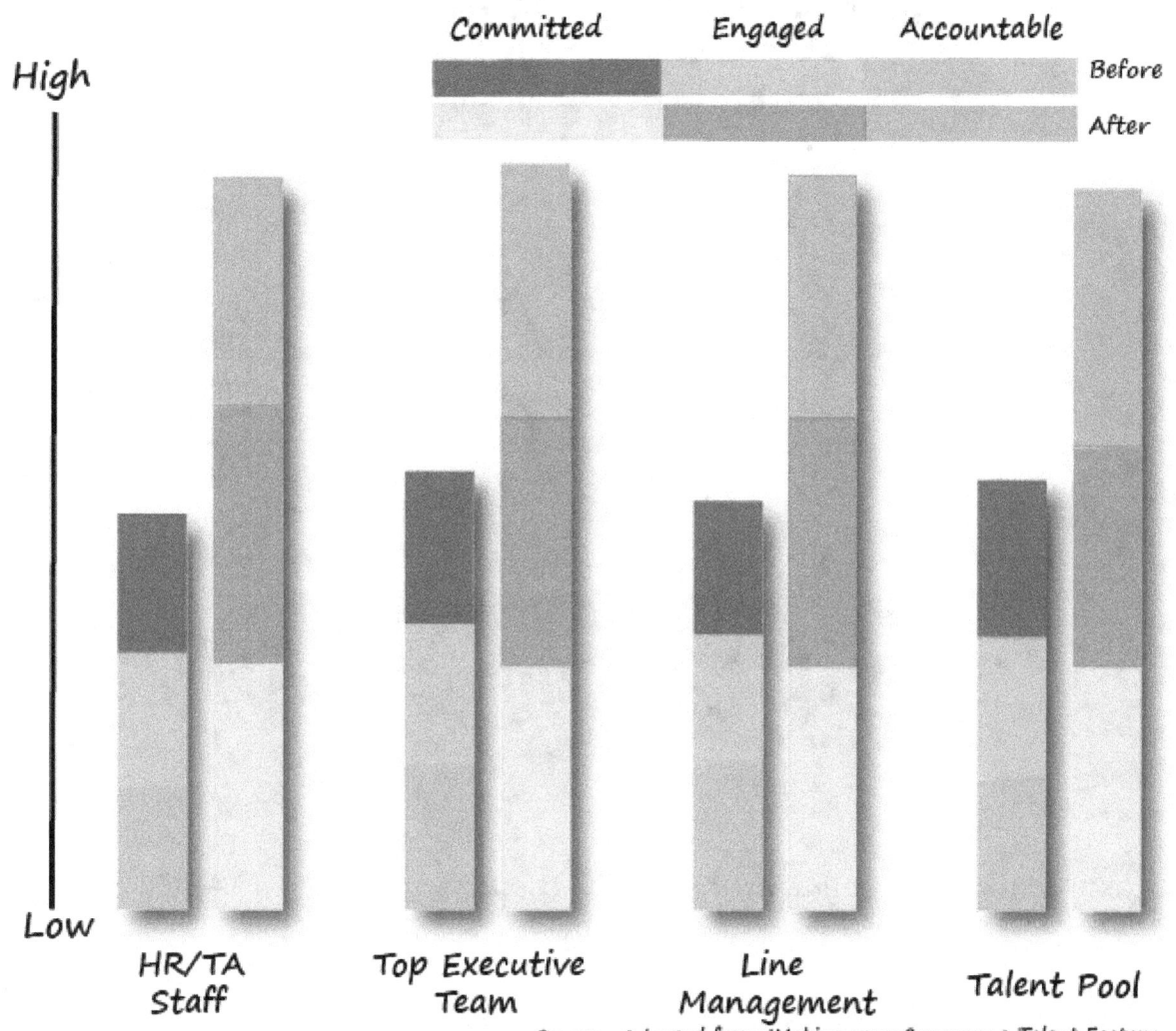

Source : Adapted from 'Making your Company a Talent Factory,
Douglas A. Ready and Jay A. Conger; HBR, June 2007

The strategic elements at the heart of ABC group's new 'Talent Acquisition

Outlook' are profiled in the Exhibit below

Readers will be able to identify some of the best practices of ABC recruiting

department around these core elements in the sections to follow

10.1 Best Practices – Recruiting Department Structure

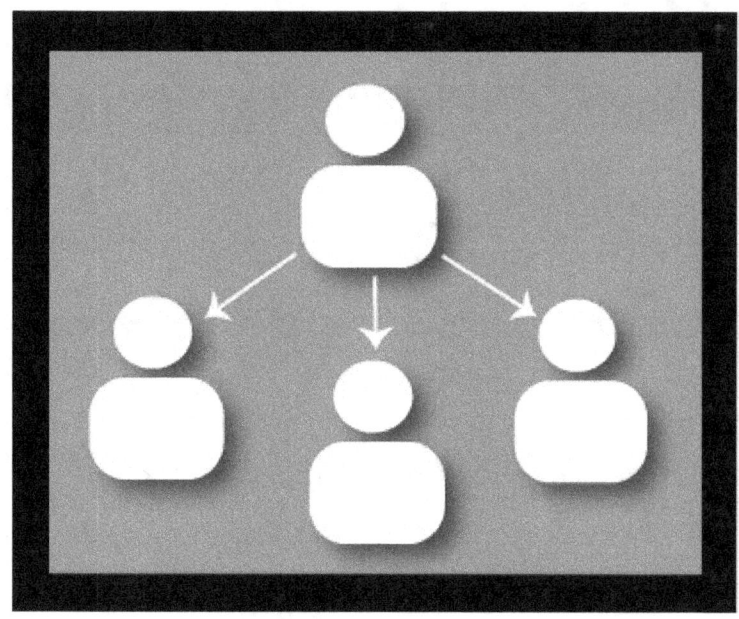

The structure of an organization defines its realities and meaning, not only in terms of personalities (who reports to whom), but in terms of texture, form, flexibility, and duration[18]. The TA and HR leaders at ABC applied the principles of leverage, specialization, customization and customer relationship management – **see Exhibit below** – in laying down the new organization form of its recruiting department

---

[18] "Straight from the CEO", G. William Dauphinais and Colin Price, Price Water House Coopers, Simon and Schuster Inc, 1998

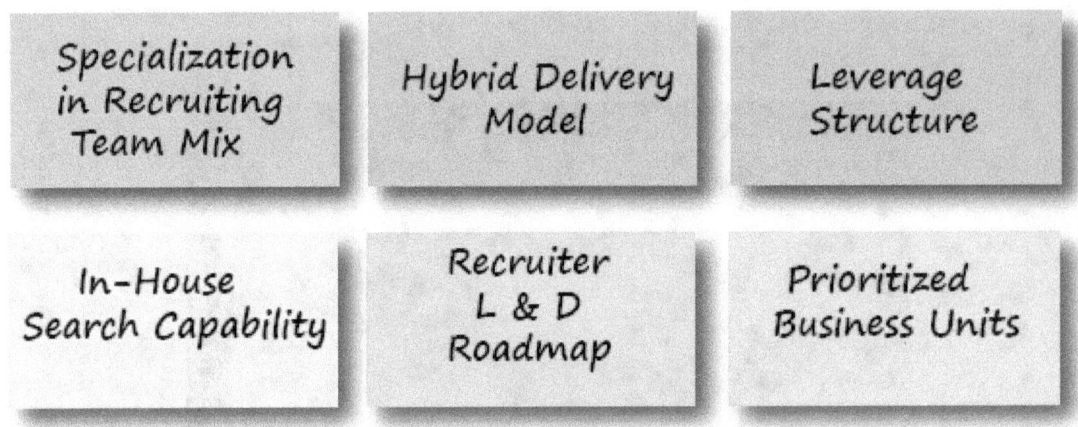

The best practices around the basic building blocks of this structure are profiled in the following section(s)

With varying refinements of language, the **mission**[19] of most Talent acquisition business units such as the one envisaged at ABC was:

> TO DELIVER
> OUTSTANDING CLIENT SERVICE
> TO PROVIDE
> FULFILLING CAREERS AND PROFESSIONAL SATISFACTION
> FOR ITS TEAM MEMBERS
> TO ACHIEVE
> FINANCIAL SUCCESS SO THAT IT CAN REWARD ITSELF
> AND GROW

---

[19] Adapted from ' A question of balance', Managing the professional services firm, David Maister, Simon & Schuster, 1993S

The Talent Acquisition function thus must satisfy three goals of "service, satisfaction, and success", if it is to build a sustainable character

refer Exhibit below

Client Satisfaction
(Service)

Profitability
(Success)

Market for Staff
(Satisfaction)

In the background of this context, managing the Talent Acquisition function at ABC required a delicate balancing act between the talent demands of its constituent group companies, the realities of the people marketplace and the firm's economic ambitions. Many factors played a role in bringing these goals into harmony, but one had a preeminent position: the ratio of junior, middle level, and senior staff in the Talent Acquisition team, referred to here as the **leverage structure presented in the exhibit below.** By leveraging its high cost seniors with low cost juniors, **TACOE** reduced its cost to the clients while simultaneously generating additional profit for the group. Striking an optimum balance between the proportion of juniors to seniors, strengthened **TACOE'** client appeal by lowering its service delivery costs.

```
        ┌─────────────────────┐
        │   Hiring Managers   │
        │      (Service)      │
        └─────────────────────┘
                   ▲
        ┌─────────────────────┐
        │      Type of        │
        │   Hiring Mandates   │
        └─────────────────────┘
                   ▲
   ┌───────────────────────────────────┐
   │        Leverage Structure         │
   └───────────────────────────────────┘
           ▲                   ▲
  ┌─────────────────┐   ┌─────────────────┐
  │      Cost       │   │     Career      │
  │       &         │   │  Opportunities  │
  │   Fee Levels    │   │                 │
  └─────────────────┘   └─────────────────┘
           ▲                   ▲
  ┌─────────────────┐   ┌─────────────────┐
  │  Profitability  │   │     Market      │
  │    (Success)    │   │    for Staff    │
  │                 │   │ (Satisfaction)  │
  └─────────────────┘   └─────────────────┘
```

The leverage structure was at the centre of the execution strategy and was reflected in the way the recruiting team at ABC was structured to fulfill the varied nature of hiring mandates. It strived to achieve an optimum allocation that was a function of four major variables:

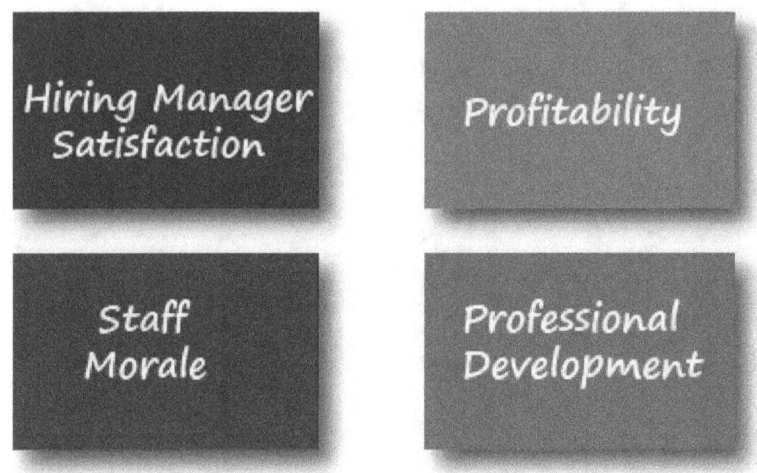

The operational outline was to follow a scheduling system that ensured that all hiring engagements are managed by a team assembled on **real** Assignment skill requirements, **real** capabilities and **real** developmental needs,

The Exhibit(s) below 20 below detail the spectrum of hiring assignments at ABC and a typical client hiring assignment scheduling system conceived in structuring the TA team at ABC group.

Hiring Spectrum- ABC Group
Representative Hiring Mandates

Brains

Procedure

Diagnosis Intensive
High Customization
High Organization Risk
High Cost

Grey Hair

Execution Intensive
Programmatic
Low Risk
Low Cost

---

20 Adapted from 'Managing The Professional Services Firm', David Maister; Simon & Schuster-1997

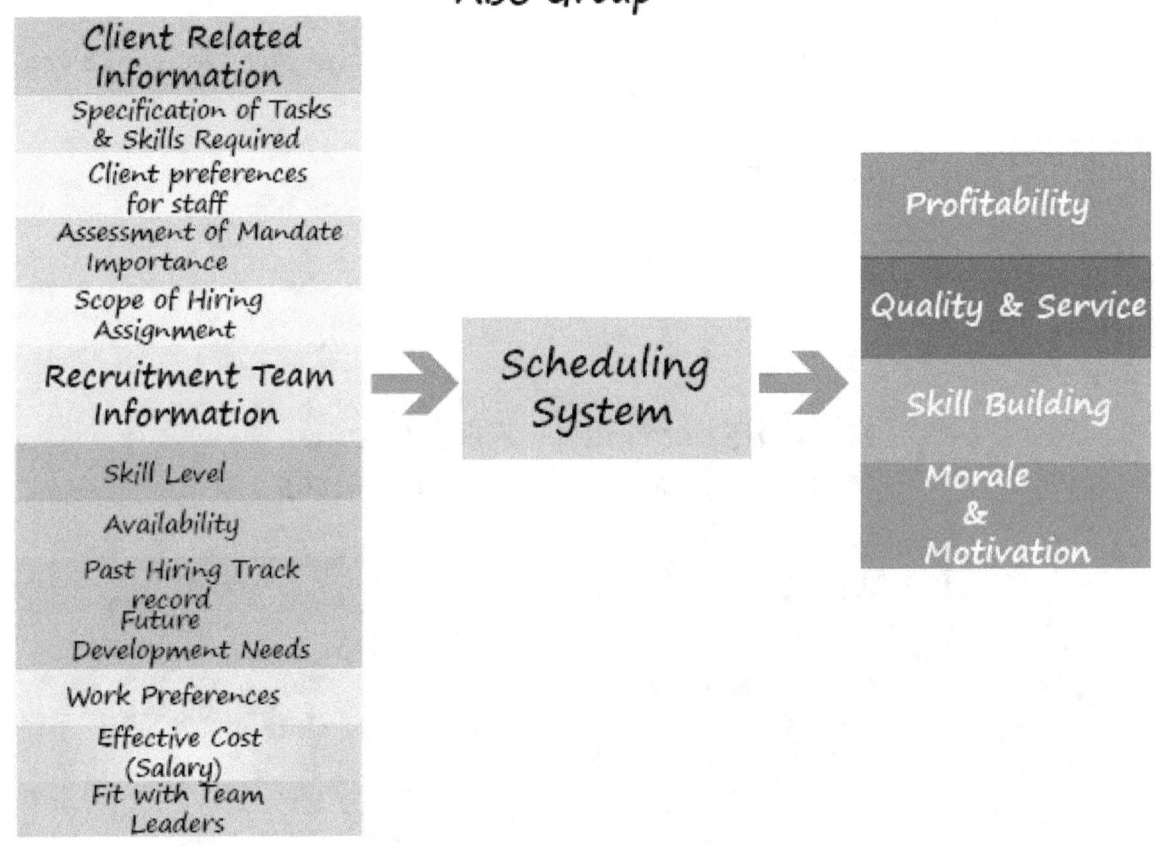

Team Structure for a Typical Hiring Assignment
ABC Group

Client Related Information
- Specification of Tasks & Skills Required
- Client preferences for staff
- Assessment of Mandate Importance
- Scope of Hiring Assignment

Recruitment Team Information
- Skill Level
- Availability
- Past Hiring Track record
- Future Development Needs
- Work Preferences
- Effective Cost (Salary)
- Fit with Team Leaders

Scheduling System

- Profitability
- Quality & Service
- Skill Building
- Morale & Motivation

Scheduling has long term consequences. Over time, the pattern of hiring mandates given to the recruitment team members profoundly influenced their professional development, their value proposition to the talent acquisition team and to the hiring managers, their satisfaction with the organization, and, as a result their motivation and productivity. Viewed as a connected set of decisions, a judicious scheduling, allocation system played a larger role in dissemination of expertise throughout the team, acting as a primary vehicle for converting the experience and knowledge of these individuals into the experience & knowledge of ABC recruiting function as a whole. The model also helped gauge the internal training requirements of the recruiting staff and accordingly draw up a learning & development roadmap for individual recruiters. In optimizing the training & development inputs to recruiters, selection criteria of the core recruiting staff played a vital role. Technology, branding, metrics are primary drivers of recruiting, and these, along with business acumen were the primary criteria for selecting the recruiting team members. A strong sense of initiative, high energy levels, an ability to thrive in pressure situations and attention-to-detail- an attitude that is essential to handle client servicing with a sense of empathy- were key personal characteristics assessed in potential recruits. The Leverage Structure discussed above also enabled creation of an In-House Candidate Search Model. The model envisaged creation of an Internal Head-Hunter role within the sourcing team (different from internal "recruiters") for its proven efficacy for leadership hires. This approach was also in sync with the TA goal of becoming a more analytic, strategic business partner by on-boarding the best talent **in** the market as against the talent available **on** the market. The **chart below** illustrates, in theory, the potential value of internal headhunting in relation to other candidate sourcing methods. It also introduces the relationship between the actual cost of the hire, with the potential value of hire.

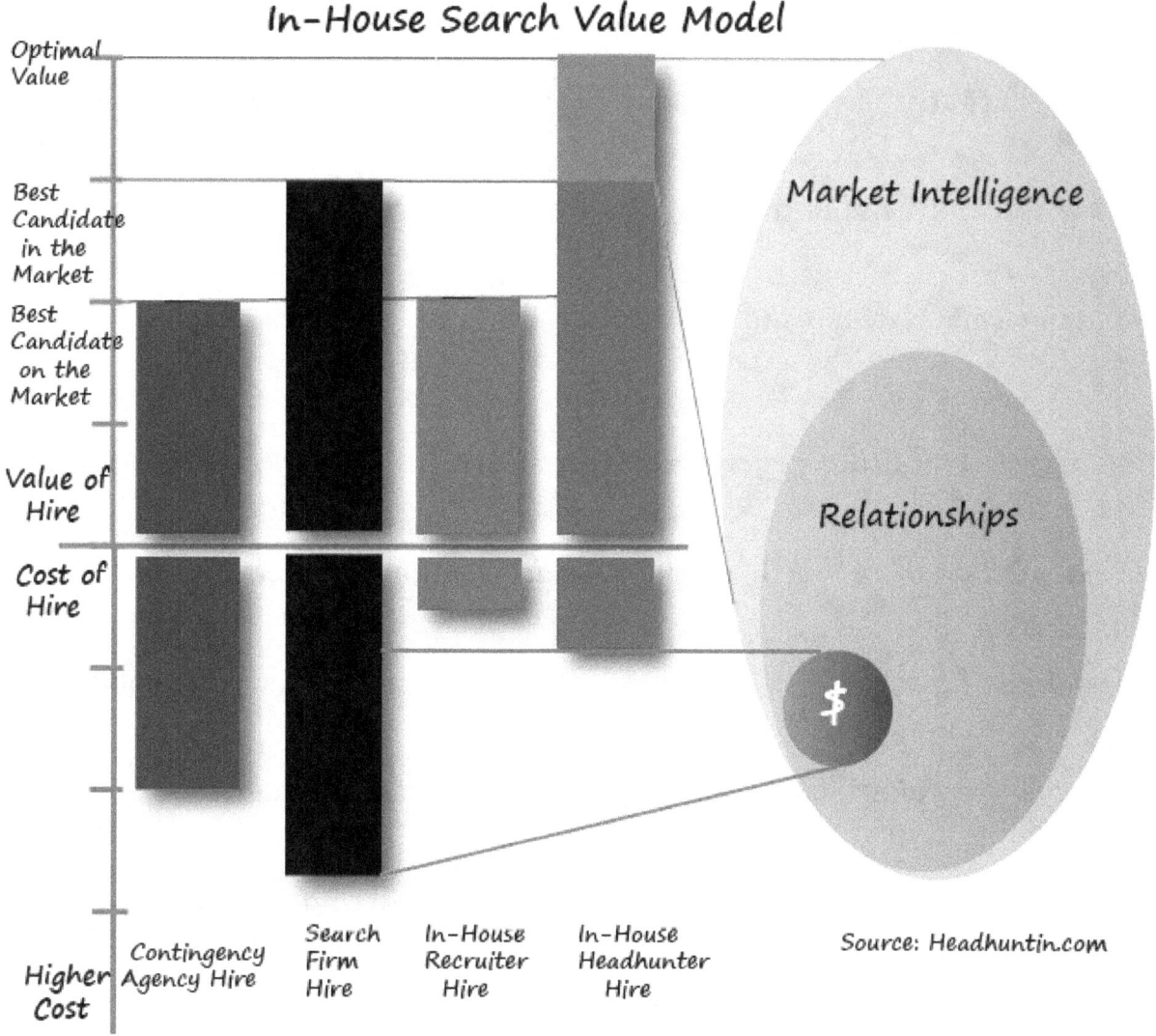

In-House Search Value Model

Source: Headhuntin.com

The in-house search role not only helped ABC in building rapport and relationships directly with the marketplace but also gather valuable market intelligence. This market intelligence could relate to the role being hired for or may serve as useful information that the business can use to its

175

advantage. Over time the search model can build on the market knowledge, get closer to the competition and ultimately increase the probability of finding the best candidate in the market for every role, not just the best of the active candidates in the market.

The overall recruiting organization structure at ABC group resembled a hybrid model where much of the recruiting effort was characterized as a centralized function. The centralized recruiting not only included the traditional recruiters but also team members with a specialist focus in the areas of branding, technology, analytics, sourcing. Additionally the recruiting department also developed a system to "customize" how it delivers on its service offerings. This was based on the unique needs of each business units and had dedicated recruiters assigned by business division in their areas of expertise.

The **Exhibit(s) below** highlight the salient aspects of the ABC TA Centre of Excellence structure and business focus

Organogram - Talent Acquisition COE

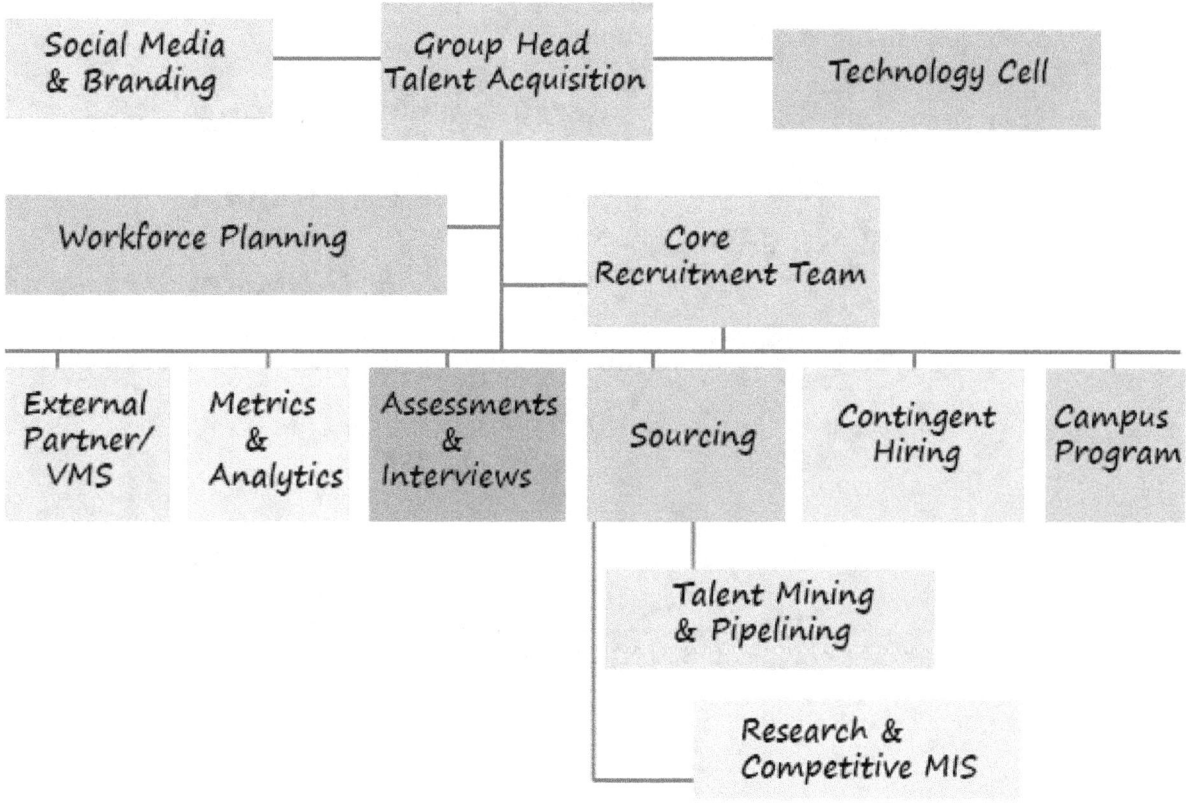

ABC Group - Talent Acquisition Strategy Focus

Workforce Planning

Assessments & Interviewing

Hiring Process Management

Direct Sourcing

Onboarding & Assimilation

Focus Streams

Metrics & Analytics

Recruitment Marketing

Social Media & Branding

Talent Pipelining

Recruiter L & D Roadmap

Waste Management DTU

Infrastructure DTU

Construction DTU

Pharma DTU

DTU - Dedicated Team Units

The new look TA organization structure at ABC had positive implications for its overall talent strategy, which included among others:

A	Talent competencies centered around multi-function process oriented skills
B	Talent strategies & initiatives delivered through a combination of Corporate & SBU levels
C	Judicious mix of permanent & temporary talent employment
D	Reduced barriers for Talent deployment
E	Talent growth & development opportunities centered on projects
F	Clearly defined and logial points of entry for new and experienced talent

The **key and most impactful** areas of optimization effected around the TA structure are profiled below:

Goals Cascading

Role Clarification

Communication Flow

Skill Alignment & Specialization

Role Duplication

Team Governance

> If you can't describe what you are doing as a process, you don't know what you're doing
>
> **W. Edwards Deming**

ABC Group - Talent Acquisition Process Outline Key Components

The ABC recruiting department implemented well defined process imperatives at each stage of the recruiting life cycle to minimize time to productivity and maximize the quality of hire. The Process & Technology section in Chapter 6.0 underscored the fact that the end customers – the hiring managers and the talent prospect – of the recruiting process are more concerned about the quality & timelines of the process outcomes than with the intervening process steps. In the customers seat recruiting services only have visibility and value if they improve customers' lives or contribute to customer success[21]. Given this context it was imperative that ABC group's repertoire of recruiting processes were strategy-ready in managing the talent flow — the right people at the right time with the needed competencies. The difference, much more than semantic, was organizing work both across the recruitment function and across the range of other business functions.

Exhibit(s) below highlight the business functional areas at ABC realigned to processes and other salient aspects of their Best Practices — Recruiting Process Strategy approach

---

[21] Adapted from "Successful Talent Strategies", David Sears; Amacom publication

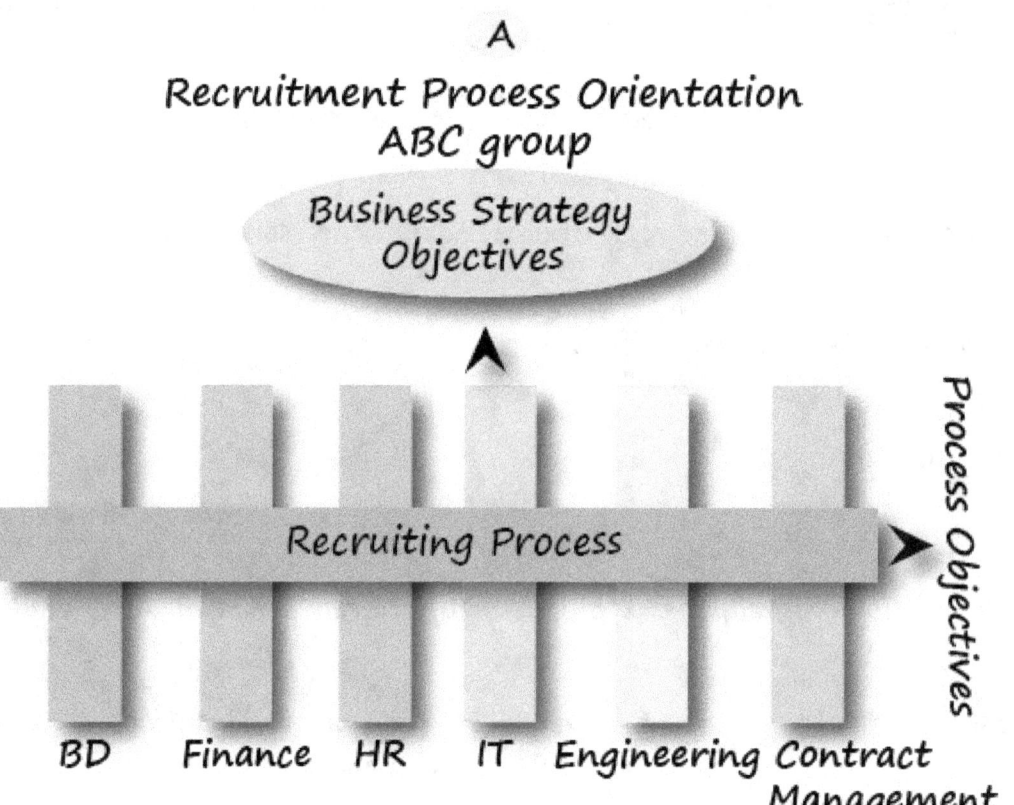

A
Recruitment Process Orientation
ABC group

B
Recruitment Process Life Cycle

Workforce Analytics	
Future Talent and Workforce priorities	Implications for sourcing and recruiting

Sourcing	
Internal Vs External	Business Needs & Criticality of roles

Acquisition	
Sourcing Channels	Partners, Job boards, referrals, campus hires, company branding

Evaluation & Selection
Assessments, cognitive & behavioral tests, structured interviews, offer extension process

Onboarding & Assimilation

C
Hiring Process Map

Understand Position & role specs Develop a Sourcing Strategy	Identify & Evaluate Prospects	Finalize Selections & Background Checks Monitor Long Term Evaluation
Understanding Client org structure Discuss & Freeze Job & Person Profile	Sourcing Plan, Screening Questionnaire & Acquisition	Interview, assess & assist in formalization of hire
Discuss Compensation & Grade particulars	Engage & Evaluate prospects on predefined criteria Present Shortlist	Maintain lien with the prospects till onboarding & monitor integration process

D
Sample Performance SLA's
Hiring Manager Committment

All requisitioned positions to be supported by formal organogram, manpower requisition forms, job/role briefs with appropriate sign-offs

Utillize the online MSS portal for all staffing resume reviews, requests and applicant processing

Work with recruiting team to develop on-line prescreen questionnaire, screening process and interview strategy

Staffing Committment

Recruiting Team, within 48 hrs of the position request would put up a specific sourcing strategy, assigignment plan, sourcing channel mix & formal jd/role specs

Based on the formal go ahead and buy-in with the HM, recruiting team would guarantee shortlist presentation of top candidates within 8 days

Based on HM shortlist, recruiting team guarantees to screen all candidates within 48 hrs in line with the job/role fitment aspects

Recruiting Team would guarantee a 24 hr response time to any HM request pertinent to hiring assignment/applicant specifics

Recruiting Team would guarantee all onboarding formalities to be completed within seven days of an incumbents joining

Recruiting Team would guarantee to publish a monthly workflow MIS document capturing all pertinent recruitment data points to enable a "quick read" on the hiring situation & align efforts accordingly

The ABC recruiting team understood that hiring managers do not always respect or give high priority to the recruiting function and accordingly developed a significant number of service level agreements with line managers. These agreements built confidence among hiring managers that recruiting will come good on its promises and was used as a positive reinforcement tool rather than an enforcement tool engendering a climate of mutual trust and goodwill to achieve the hiring objectives.

Sample Assignment Plan
RACI Matrix

Activity	Process Partners		Timelines	Remarks
	Recruiting Team & HR	Hiring Manager		
HM Intake Mtg	RAI	RA		
Mandate confirmation	RI	RA		
Freeze job/role specs	RAI	RA		
Sourcing Strategy	RA	I		
Execution Kick Off	RA	I		
Prel. Screening shortlist	RA	A		
Interview Sch	RA	RA		
Selections	RC	RA		
Ref Checks	RA	I		
Offer Roll out	RCI	RA		
Onboarding	RA	I		

R - Responsible
A - Accountable
I - Informed
C - Consulted

Integration of the above process elements in the recruitment strategy at ABC underscored the importance of the need for both Hiring Managers and Talent Acquisition team to work as a well knit cohesive unit.

Recent research[22] uncovered that

Developing strong relationships with hiring managers is the top driver of talent acquisition performance

This finding is also supported by the fact that hiring managers take most of the workload during the candidate selection phase.

Please refer Exhibit below to view this excerpt from an Industry leading Recruiting Roundtable Study[23]

---

[22] "High Impact Talent Acquisition – Key Findings & Maturity Model", Bersin by Deloitte, September, 2014

[23] Recruiting Roundtable, *The State of the Recruiting Function*, Corporate Executive Board (January 2006)

Ownership of Activities in the Candidate Selection Phase

	Application Collection	Selection of Whom to Interview	Candidate Interviewing	Selection of Whom to Hire
Recruiters	75%	38%	34.7%	4.2%
HR Generalists	4.2%	4.2%	1.4%	1.4%
Admn Assts	5.6%	0%	0%	0%
Hiring Managers	0%	49.3%	58.3%	88.9%
Others	8.2%	5.7%	4.2%	5.5%

Lean Supply Chain Tools in Recruiting

The Process & Technology section in Chapter 4.0 examined in detail how the ABC group went about adopting the basic tenets of lean in appraising the efficacy of its recruiting process. By embracing the fundamentals of Lean Manufacturing — identifying value-creating activities, eliminating waste, and focusing on continuous improvement — TA & HR leaders at ABC realized that they could lift recruitment to new heights of efficiency and quality. Further, the initiative also gave business stakeholders more insight on the internals of the recruiting process and its ability to make a visible

bottom-line impact. The Exhibit(s) below capture the salient aspects of the

re-engineered recruiting process and the areas of impact across the ABC

talent supply chain.

Value Stream Map- Re-engineered Recruitment Process: ABC Group

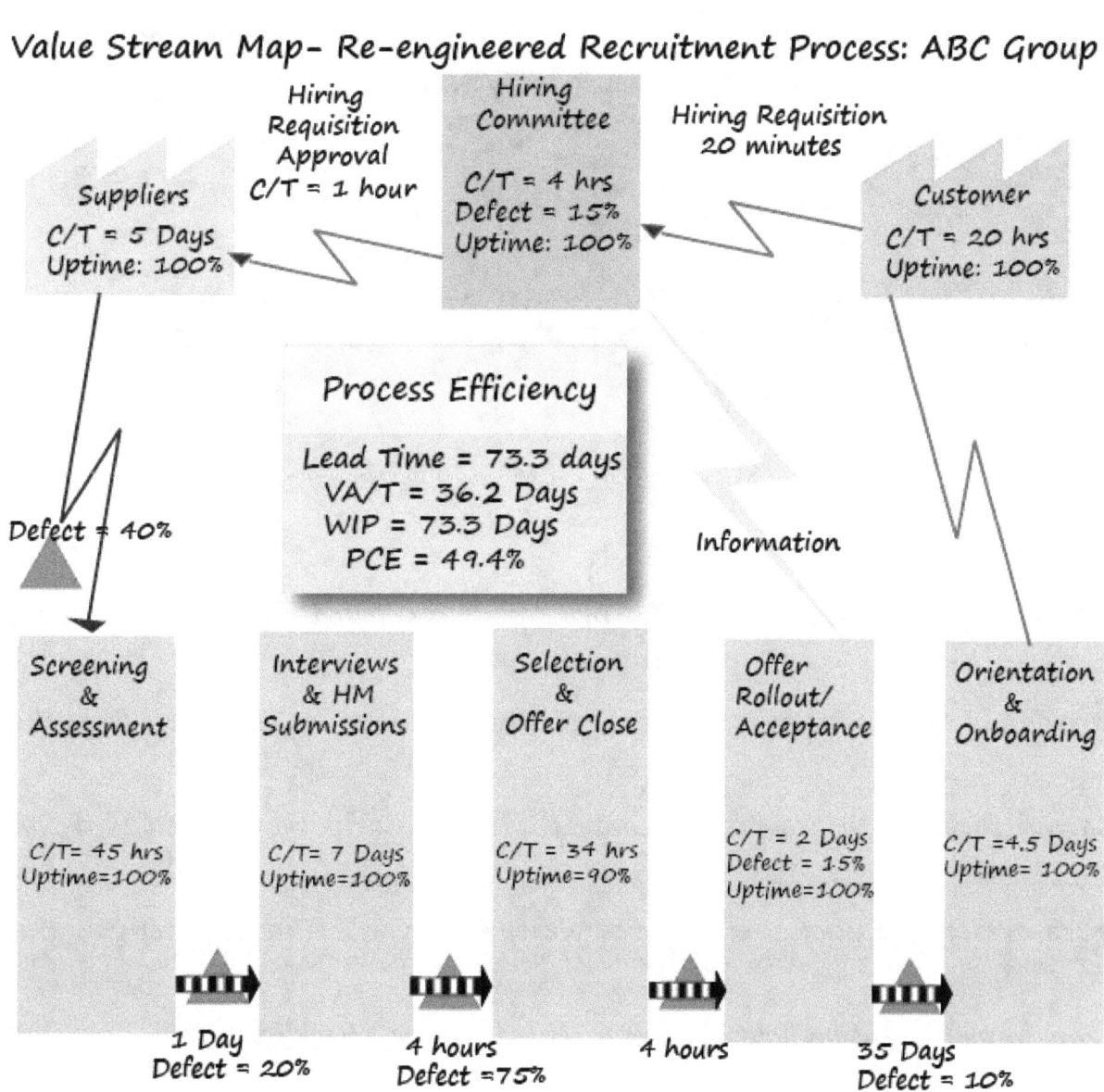

ABC Talent Supply Chain: Area of Impact

- Recruiter Process Efficiency Improvement
- Administrative Process Efficiency Improvement
- Hiring Manager Process Efficiency Improvement
- Offline Advertising Expense Reduction
- External Partners Fee Reduction
- New Hire Travel and Relocation Expense Reduction
- Reduction in External Hire Time to Fill
- Reduction in Time to Onboarding for New External Hires
- Internal Mobility Ratio Improvement
- Staffing Consistency

Ultimately, the lean tools and principles employed at ABC was about providing smart, deliverable data to the business stakeholders and then saying to them, 'Here are not only the benchmarks we started with, but here are the additional efficiencies we can deliver.' The key steps in their lean implementation journey are profiled in the **checklist below**. The same could serve as a template for organizations looking to put their priorities

and lean plan into action and achieve operational excellence in recruitment.

Lean Recruitment Journey - ABC Group

Identify Value	Defining value from the perspective of end customers – Hiring Managers, Candidates, external partners-
Map the Value Stream	Value stream mapping the current and future state recruiting process. Identified and categorized waste in the current state followed by its elimination
Create Value	Creating flow by organizing work and team environment (5S); Created Kaizen, change management teams & visual management tools to eliminate functional barriers and improve lead times
Establish Pull	A Pull based strategy of providing hiring managers /clients with the right candidates at the right time with the right skillset and the right price. Primary focus on tapping into 'raw material'' candidate inventory and qualify & deliver a talent pool in direct response to a hiring need
Seek Perfection	Value streaming the process and repeating again focusing on continuous improvement

Source: Adapted from " The Five Steps of Lean Implementation, www.lean.org

Green Recruiting: Reduced Paper & Processing Costs
Increased Employment Brand Equity

eRecruiting

Direct Cost Savings

SaaS based
Cloud Recruiting Products

Low Carbon Footprint

Employee Benefits

Holistic Health Options
Paid Volunteer Time for
Environment causes

Green Recruiting
Integral to ABC Group's
Value Statement

Good Environment Citizenship
Employment Branding

ABC Group's **Green Bias** in recruiting was a natural extension of its business

presence in the **environment management space**. Awarded the "Best

Company" for two years in the running for market leadership in the Industrial Waste Management domain in India, the group's environmental stance was a critical element of its sales pitch to potential applicants and candidates. Making **"greenness"** an important element of its employment brand also helped the group attract more of the Gen Y and College grads – a generation which has grown up with a "green mindset", learning about environment & recycling since elementary school – for its entry level volume hiring. Automating the recruitment work flow and information flows – and making it green led to direct cost savings.. These savings came from reduced paperwork related to resumes, advertising, and on-boarding. Additionally, integration of a Software-as-a-Service (SaaS) e-recruiting software in its Talent Acquisition system, which is inherently greener than purchased software running on local servers, helped create a redundant computing environment with smaller carbon footprints.

These best practices around ABC' recruiting process redesign significantly increased the overall effectiveness, efficiency and utilization of resources to maximize the quality of its hires. Business process redesign, contrary to popular belief, is not a mere automation of tasks to reduce cycle time or human effort[24]. It transcends to the identification of non-value adding activities in a process that can be obliterated to achieve dramatic improvements in critical, contemporary measures of performance such as cost, quality, service and speed[25].

The ABC group recruiting process redesign initiative was testimony to this precept

---

[24] Hammer, M. (1990), "Reengineering Work; Don't Automate, Obliterate," HBR, July/August, pp. 104-112

[25] Hammer, M., Champy. J., (1993), "Reengineering the Corporation: A Manifesto for Business Revolution.", Harper Collins, London

10.3 Best Practices – Workforce Planning Process

> " Life is what happens to you while you are busy making other plans!"
>
> John Lennon

The Leadership team at ABC probably drew a cue from this famous John Lennon line in their workforce optimization effort. The **Workforce – Planning** process in the COE model elevated recruiting effectiveness to a new level at **ABC group**. It was a key weapon in their recruiting arsenal and helped provide predictive, precision forecasting in direct contrast to the earlier straight line, historical based constant growth rate forecasting planning model – **Please refer Exhibit below** – This traditional workforce planning model more resembled the Dodge Dart of the 1960s and '70s – a basic, get–you-there model without any bells and whistles. While a reliable and functional model, the changing business environment and demands of a global business necessitated a forecasting model better aligned with the strategic business planing and budgeting exercise at ABC.

Workforce Planning Process: Traditional Approach

Define Objectives	Project Demand	Evaluate Supply	Define Gaps	Gap Management
Gather data from the business plan or business strategy to determine the direction of the workforce plan	Qualitative analysis to determine key needs	Quantitative analysis of critical employee data elements	Define and prioritize the gaps between qualitative demand and quantitative supply	Develop action plan to close gaps
	Headcount Financial Marketing Risk Mgmt			Build Buy Borrow Bounce

The new model integrated elements of Workforce Analytics, Segmentation, and Scenario-Modelling and enabled **ABC** to pinpoint with precision its staffing needs and develop staffing supply chains, training programs and succession plans in accordance and to meet its future business needs at least three years in advance. A distinguishing feature of the model was an

interactive forecasting method which relied on detailed interactions with all key business stakeholders and their workgroup units. This helped generate sharper insights factoring multiple scenarios around the workforce forecasts. Similar to the Delphi Method, it was based on the assumption that group judgments are more valid than individual judgments. The workforce planning also served as a competitive weapon by tracking the market and gaining insights on key competitor activity. The process in particular factored in a host of qualitative variables that were never part of the previous model:

- Industry Trends

- Changes in Labor & Employment laws

- Political Developments — both local and overseas markets

- New Business Strategies

The Exhibit(s) below capture the salient aspects of the model. A **Sample Workforce PlanningTemplate** employed at ABC to project hiring needs based on terminations, expected retirements, and projected growth needs is also presented below. The same was benchmarked factoring Industry research data[26] around workforce planning best practices

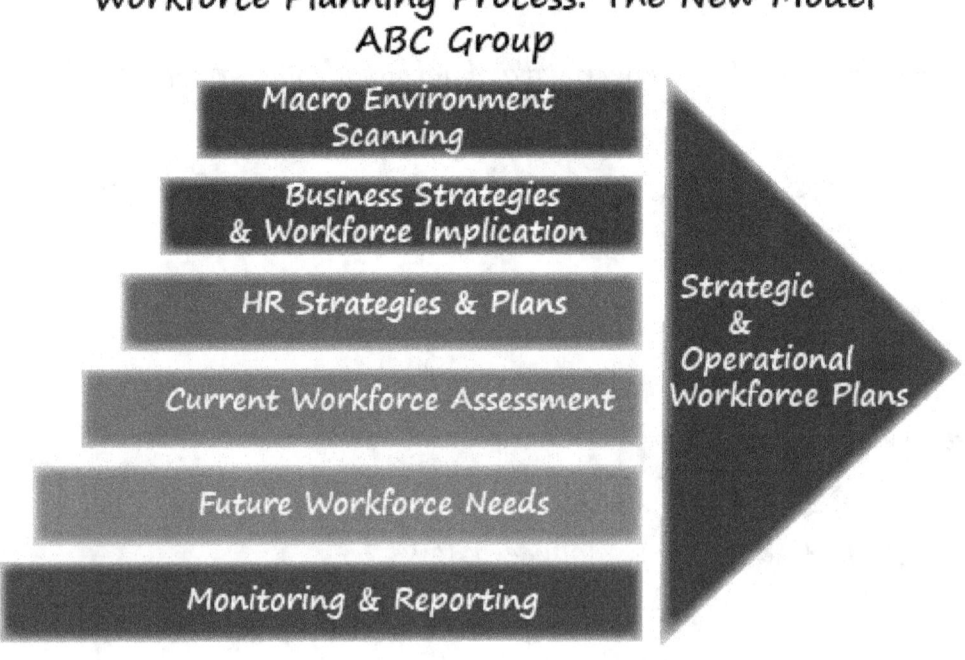

Workforce Planning Process: The New Model
ABC Group

Macro Environment Scanning

Business Strategies & Workforce Implication

HR Strategies & Plans

Current Workforce Assessment

Future Workforce Needs

Monitoring & Reporting

Strategic & Operational Workforce Plans

---

[26] Journal of Corporate Recruiting Leadership | crjournal.com | August'2007

Unit Level Staffing Plans – Base Model

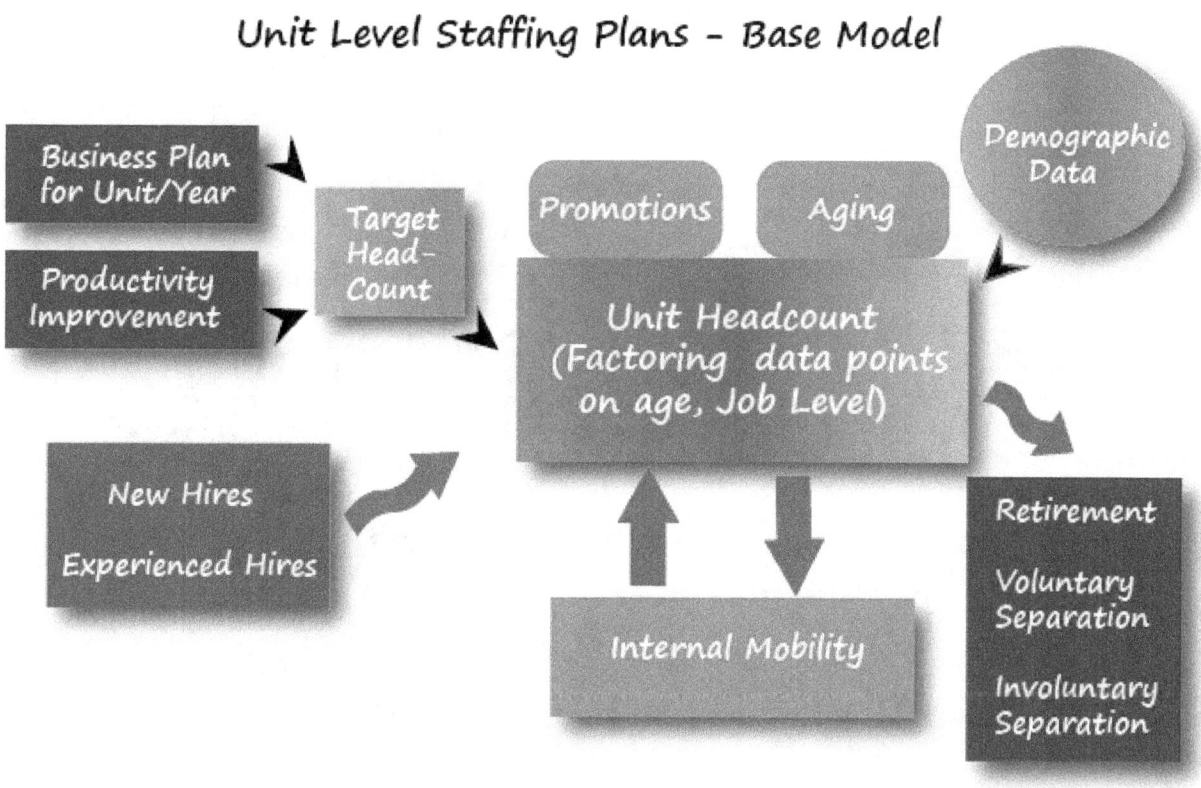

Workforce Planning Components

Sample Template : Annual Workforce Planning Tool

A. New Initiative/ Key Business Change
(Non- Business - as - usual staffing drivers)

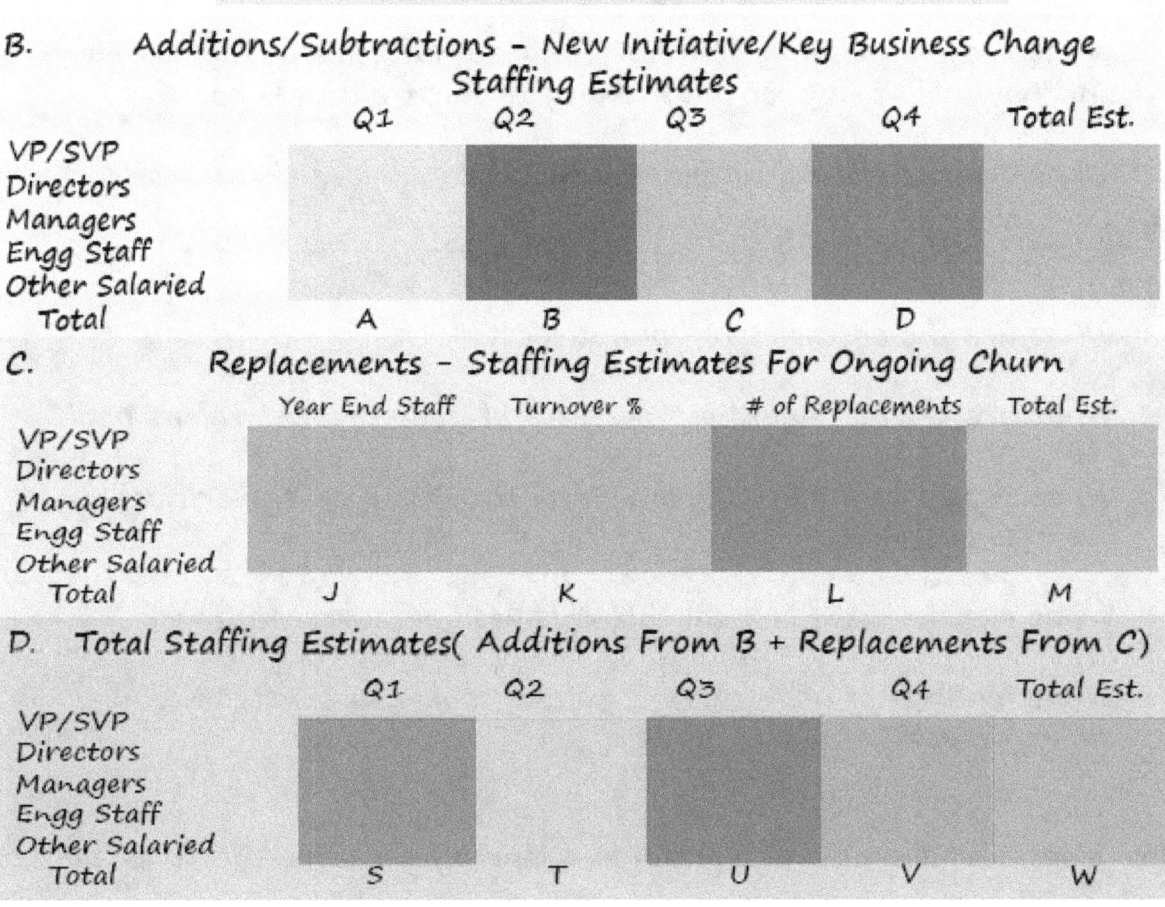

Market Expansion

Process Improvement

New Projects Bid Conversion

B. Additions/Subtractions - New Initiative/Key Business Change
Staffing Estimates

	Q1	Q2	Q3	Q4	Total Est.
VP/SVP					
Directors					
Managers					
Engg Staff					
Other Salaried					
Total	A	B	C	D	

C. Replacements - Staffing Estimates For Ongoing Churn

	Year End Staff	Turnover %	# of Replacements	Total Est.
VP/SVP				
Directors				
Managers				
Engg Staff				
Other Salaried				
Total	J	K	L	M

D. Total Staffing Estimates(Additions From B + Replacements From C)

	Q1	Q2	Q3	Q4	Total Est.
VP/SVP					
Directors					
Managers					
Engg Staff					
Other Salaried					
Total	S	T	U	V	W

Sample Template – Interactive Forecasting Method
Key Business Stakeholders

What are the key business goals and objectives for the next year?

What are the key business trends influencing your business unit?

What are the primary sources of our competitive advantage and how will it impact your ability to meet business goals?

What are the critical processes needed to achieve these goals?

What are the key success factors for achieving future outcomes?

What are the obstacles to your success?

What are the distinguishing features of your present talent pool?

What people capabilities are needed to deliver on the critical business outcomes?

What are the most critical talent issues you currently face?

What features of your current talent pool may constrain your ability to achieve future success?

The biggest challenge to workforce planning, which ABC was able to overcome was to get its leadership to believe that it is an organization initiative and not a HR or a TA intervention.

The leadership commitment to invest the time, money and effort helped

realize the benefits of the most appropriate workforce planning techniques.

Analytical workforce planning processes centered around expert forecasting,

scenario planning, extrapolation techniques formed the core of the ABC

Workforce Forecast model enabling it to work into the future with the most

optimized workforce within its business context.

> There is nothing more satisfying than providing a service and demonstrating its value with systematically collected data

A business organization without financial measures such as earnings growth, cash flow, return on equity, and return on sales is unlikely to be a viable business for long. However, the focus of these measures on past results (what was) versus ongoing process (how things are working as indicators of how they might improve) may create blind spots, particularly in customer-focused strategies such as for Talent Acquisition. The **metrics and measurement section in Chapter 6.0** delved in detail on some of these pitfalls as also the fact that the most commonly used recruiting metrics are "historical metrics" with an almost universal focus on costs and process efficiency. Additionally, there is a temptation to report on too many metrics, which may have the purported effect of projecting a pretty picture but in reality they use up key resources and offer little value or business impact. Faced with numerous measurement options, the TA & HR leadership at ABC went about the task of building a high impact measurement repertoire in a purposeful, systematic, and selective manner. This approach – **Please refer Exhibit below** – ensured that both financial and process measures were considered; that different value criteria of external and internal stakeholders are taken into account; and that offsetting improvements and setbacks (short-term financial results, for example, coming at the expense of operational quality and customer relationships) were equally visible[27].

---

[27] Robert S. Kaplan and David P. Norton, The Balanced Scorecard, Translating Strategy into Action (Boson; Harvard Business School Press, 1996)

Balancing Critical & Uncontrollable	"What is critical is often not controllable, what is controllable is often not critical." The ABC TA & HR leadership looked at measures relevant to business results and which would resonate with customers. It was felt crucial to have strategies determine critical measures rather than having strategies be governed by controllable measures
Balancing "physician" and "coroner" measures	The fundamental language of business is about both work achievement and money. While businesses need a strong balance sheet and P&L, these describe specific outcomes (what happened) and are lagging indicators. This needed to be balanced by real time indicators (how effectively are things happening) to have an effective measurement slate
Balancing value creation and cost reduction	Business strategies are designed to create wealth, not to cut expenses. Denominator measures - measures that exclusively emphasize cost cutting (lowering CTH or staff expenses) - will eventually create diminishing returns for most types of strategies
Balancing the needs of measurement audiences	Talent Acquisition strategies like business strategies have multiple customer audiences, including business unit leaders, hiring managers, talent prospects, current employees and talent alumni. Metrics must be relevant and meaningful to its targeted audience

With the above considerations in place, we move on next to the steps that

ABC took with a clean measurement slate[28] – as a way of auditing the

value of current process metrics (the ones which are ineffective or are

---

[28] David Sears, Successful Talent Strategies; AMACOM 2003, p. 214

redundant) and identifying missing measures – Readers may like to refer back to the metrics & measurement section in Chapter 6.0 on how the ABC TA & HR team decided to step back and rethink the measurement game in the background of a shifting talent market. The measurement slate employed the following steps:

A — Defining the factors (Time, Cost, Quality etc.) most important to process customers

B — Mapping the Recruiting Process to deliver results

C — Identifying the critical steps and competencies required for process success

D — Design measures (time, cost, quality, process results) to track these steps and competencies

The balancing considerations coupled with this clean state approach to developing TA process measures finally paved the way for a Talent Acquisition Scorecard construct graphically presented in the Exhibit below

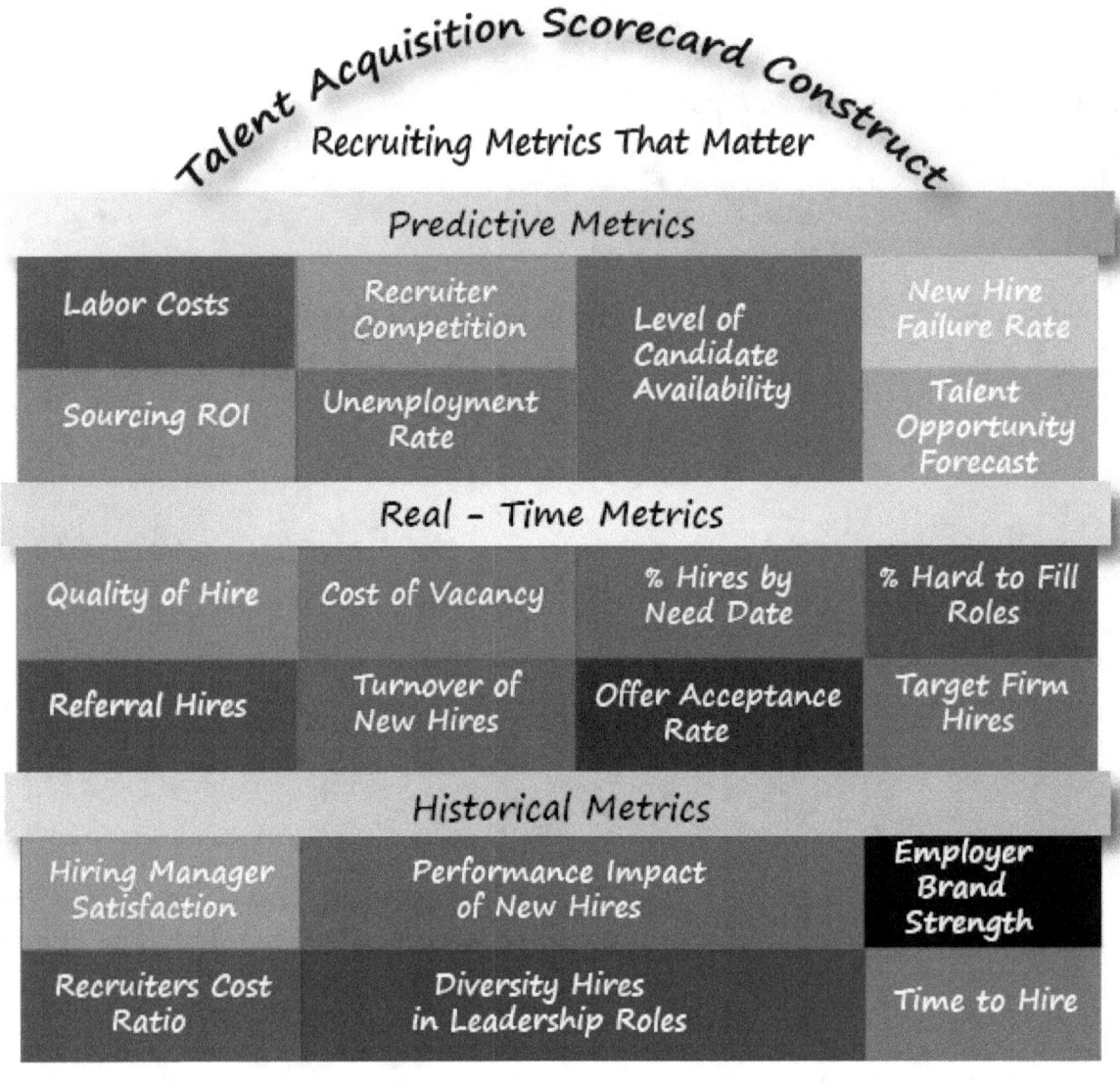

Talent Acquisition Scorecard Construct
Recruiting Metrics That Matter

Predictive Metrics

| Labor Costs | Recruiter Competition | Level of Candidate Availability | New Hire Failure Rate |
| Sourcing ROI | Unemployment Rate | | Talent Opportunity Forecast |

Real - Time Metrics

| Quality of Hire | Cost of Vacancy | % Hires by Need Date | % Hard to Fill Roles |
| Referral Hires | Turnover of New Hires | Offer Acceptance Rate | Target Firm Hires |

Historical Metrics

| Hiring Manager Satisfaction | Performance Impact of New Hires | Employer Brand Strength |
| Recruiters Cost Ratio | Diversity Hires in Leadership Roles | Time to Hire |

The predictive capability of this TA scorecard was spun around a clear understanding of the _hierarchy of knowledge about data, metrics and analytics._ The pathway to this construct was not a straight leap to analytics but a hop (data), skip (metrics) and a jump (analytics) to enable true insights in how ABC went about executing its data – driven TA strategy.

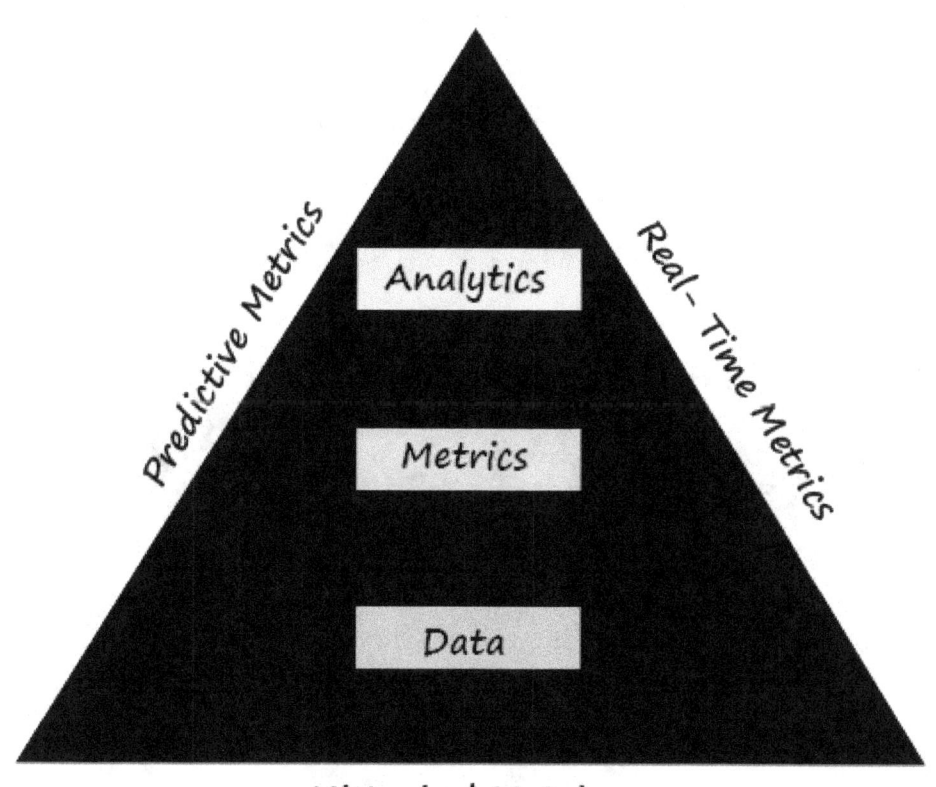

This matrix of metrics created by ABC served as a performance based measurement and management framework, linked to talent strategy which, tracked and guided action in support of acquiring, engaging and on-boarding critical organization talent. It also enabled decision makers to get a 'quick read' on the current situation and help determine where action must be taken to ensure ABC met its desired talent and business goals. The three types of metrics in the TA scorecard construct in its integrated form had one clear focus on how to impact the result of the hiring process, i.e. retention and new hire performance, which at the end of the day that is what really matters:

> Delivering Candidates who are better today than they were yesterday

We next profile in the exhibits below some key categories of reporting dashboards utilized by the ABC TA department.

Sourcing Channel Reports

Sourcing Channel Mix

Direct Sourcing	Social Media Channels	Campus Recruitments
Internal Mobility	Employee Referral Program	Online Databases & Job Postings
	External Partners	ATS/CRM

Measurement of Sourcing Channels- Key Criteria

Costs	% of Budget	% of Applicants
% of Positions Filled	Speed	Efficiency
Quality (12 mth T/O)	Vendor Dependability Scorecard	Average Salary of Positions Filled

Senior Management Reporting Dashboard

- Efficiency Metrics - Fixed & Variable
- Recruiters Cost Ratio
- Speed of Hire
- Trailing Twelve Month Turnover
- Turnover Analysis - Voluntary, Terminations
- Average Salary of Positions Filled

Process Time	Service level agreements	External Vendors Performance data
Recruiting Efficiency	Requisition Risk factor	Competitors/ Industry data
Talent Brand Index		Recruiter requisition load

10.5 Best Practices – Technology

> The first rule of any technology used in business is that automation applied to an efficient operation will magnify the efficiency. The second is that automation applied to an inefficient operation will magnify the inefficiency
>
> **BILL GATES**

The wisdom of this maxim was not lost upon on the TA leaders at ABC, who viewed new technology less as a complexity issue and more as an agent of positive change aimed at enhancing the candidate and employee experience. In reviewing its technology needs to support the recruitment optimization effort, the TA leaders at ABC took a holistic view of its entire technology ecosystem. This was considered necessary to ensure a seamless integration of all of their systems, services and applications and utilize the very best technology solution in addressing their specific recruiting challenges. In adopting a "best of breed" approach the TA & HR leaders not only looked at the individual dimensions of their enterprise technology framework, but also the way these different dimensions e.g. Information Technology Infrastructure, General Purpose Information Technologies & the Recruiting Process Information Technology would interact with each other. The same is illustrated below:

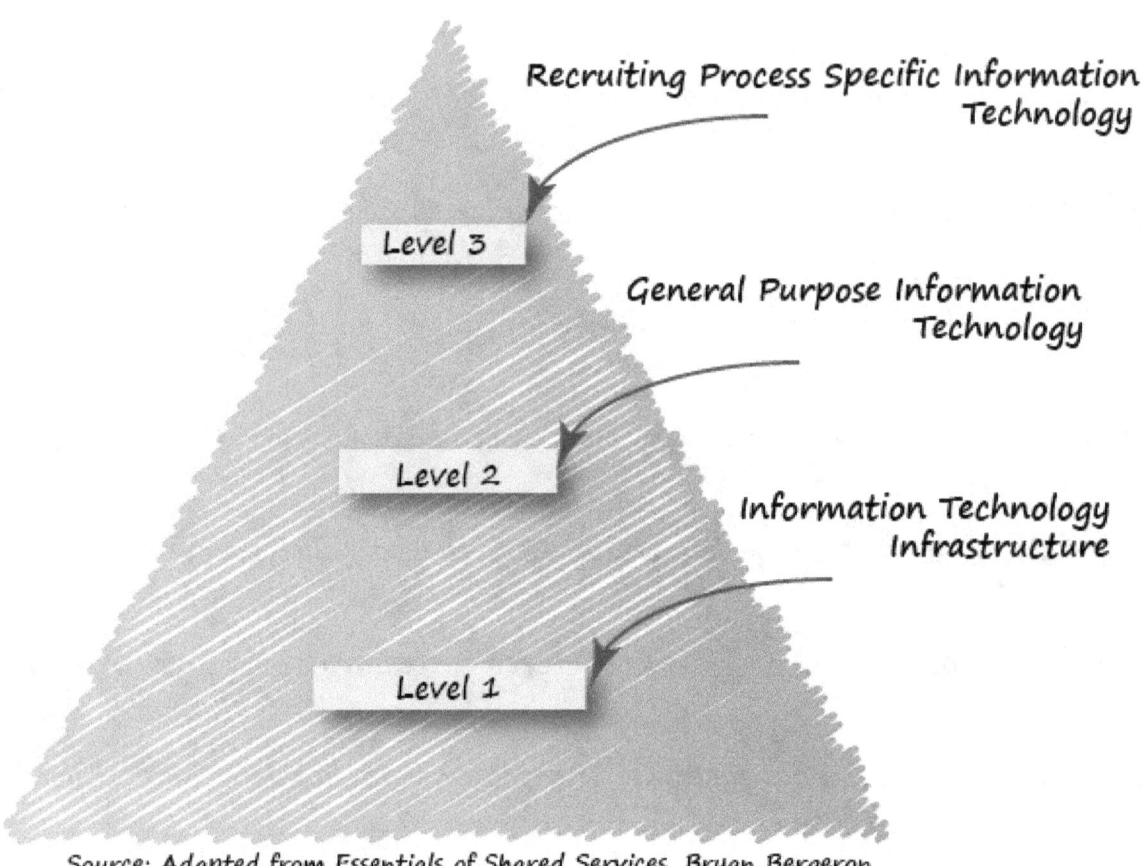

Source: Adapted from Essentials of Shared Services, Bryan Bergeron
John Wiley and Sons, Inc., 2003

The key criteria's discussed in the technology appraisal phase – please refer Chapter 6.0 – ensured that their recruiting technology platform of choice was really an "integration platform" which not only is used to track incoming resumes, but also connect to sourcing tools and services, assessment tools and services, video interviewing platforms, job boards, social media channels, external talent supply partners. Key features of this technology platform are profiled below:

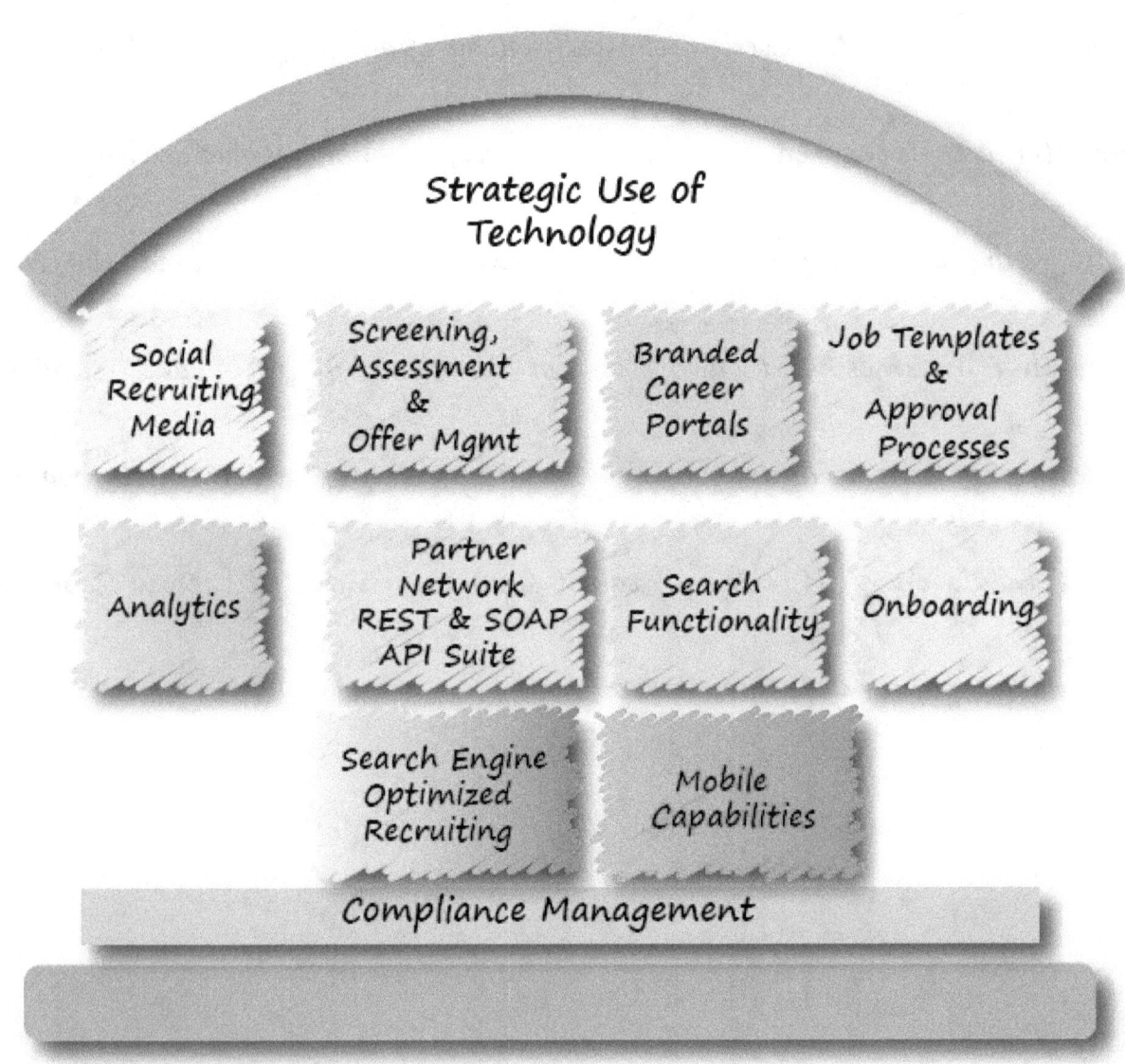

The recruiting software at the heart of the ATS implemented at ABC leveraged emerging recruitment technologies – illustrated below- based on clear business outcomes.

Integration of ATS with key Recruiting Technologies & Trends

Content and community enabled career portals	Mobile Capabilities & Social Media Integration	Understanding Data and Context	Bringing recruitment out of a silo

The recruiting industry is marked by constant change and innovation. While this provides organizations with new ways to connect and engage with top talent, keeping up with these changes can be overwhelming. But for corporate' such as ABC to remain competitive, a firm understanding of the latest market trends and leveraging on the best case technology solution offering was considered integral to its talent acquisition optimization effort.

11 Results Produced by ABC Group Recruiting Team

While laying down best practices around the strategic TA elements was a laudable effort for ABC, the real fruit of their labor was in the significant results these practices produced. The positive ROI and lowering of the total cost of ownership helped elevate the group's competitive advantage in attracting top drawer talent. The **exhibits below** showcase both the financial and strategic impact of this optimization effort.

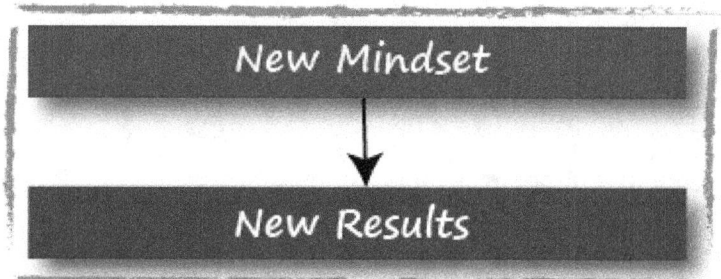

New Mindset

New Results

Quantitative Results

In-House Executive Search model & Optimized portfolio of staffing partners by 70% saved USD 300000

Cost to Hire reduced by 36.6% with a bottomline impact of USD 700000

Staffing Process efficiency leveraging Lean Supply Chain Tools improved from 18.9% to 49.4%

Improving the Recruiting Cycle time by 35% resulted in an Opportunity Cost saving of USD 10.22 million

The Throughput - maximizing on the number of quality hires increased by 40%, reflective of the quality of the recruiting team at ABC

Efficiency Analysis	Baseline	Current State
Appl per Hire/Routes Per Hire/ Offers extended to Positions Filled	245/9/82%	42/5/95
# of applications recieved (dispositioned)	188160	32256
# of candidates routed to HM for consideration	6912	4608
# of Offers extended to Candidates	937	808
Hires	768	768
Recruiter Time Savings		Annual Time Savings/Baseline
# Hours Saved by dispositioning unqualified candidates(assume 75% resume review @ 2 mts/resume		3898
Hiring Manager Time Savings		
# Hours saved by HM's Reviewing resumes(assuming 3 mts/resume)		166
# Hours saved by HM's Interviewing Candidates(assuming 50% interviews and 1 hour/interview		768
Total Hours Saved		4832
Bottom-Line Impact : USD 245460		

Staff Productivity	Baseline	Current State	% Change
Staff Productivity*	768	1075	40%

* 40% more annual hires with the same staff size

Process Efficiency	Baseline	Current State	% Change
Applicants per Hire	245	42	83%
Candidates Routed to HM per Hire	9	5	44%
Offers Extended to positions Filled %	82%	95%	13%

Sample Recruiting Cost Efficiency Measure

Assuming the following annual recruiting and staffing data for ABC Group

- No of positions filled: 1150

- Internal Costs: INR 14,200,000

- Search Project Costs: INR 49,75,000 - A

- Advertising Costs: INR 21,00,000 - B

- Relocation/Travel Expenses: INR 19,25,150 - C

- Signing/Joining Bonuses: INR 4,50,000 - D

- Average annual compensation for hires: INR 1,54,000

- External Costs: A + B + C + D = INR 94,50,150

- Total Cost: Internal Costs + External Costs = INR 23,650,150

- Total Compensation Recruited: 1150 X INR 154000 = INR 177100000

- Staffing Cost Ratio = Total Cost/Total Compensation Recruited = INR 23,650,150/INR 177,100,000 = 0.133 = 13.3%

Adapted from Staffing.org recruiting efficiency measure

Qualitative Results

Re-engineered a dispersed recruiting function to an agile, adaptable, rapidly scalable & cost effective COE model

Created a metrics driven recruiting function enabling senior executives to direct staffing initiatives & monitor their effectiveness

Elevated the status of the recruiting function from a business process to a business critical partner

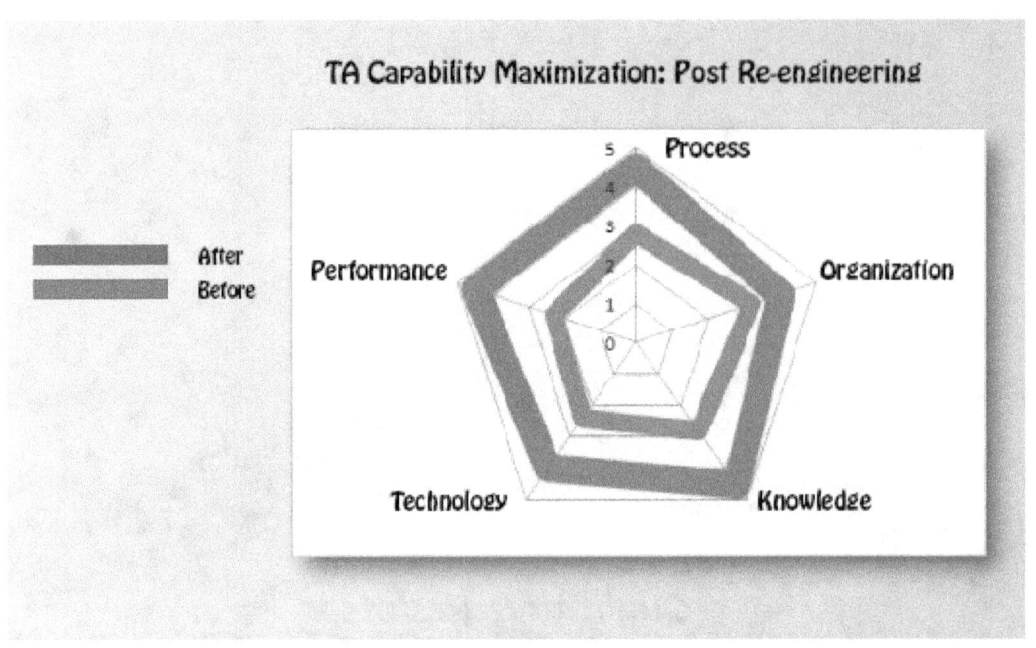

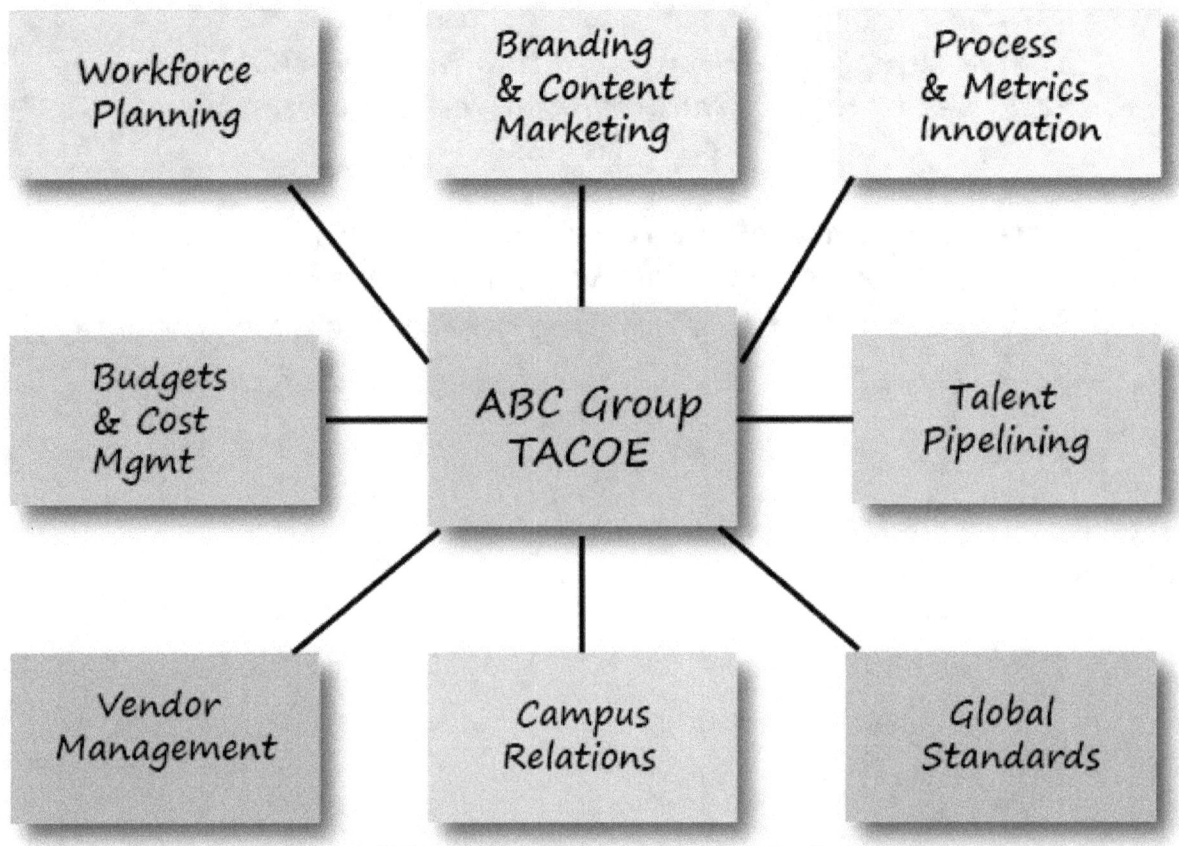

Legend: TACOE: Talent Acquisition Centre of Excellence

The technology enablement by way of introduction of a Global TAS platform involved a number of components: database building, digital marketing of opportunities, social recruiting, and other efforts. Multiple benefits included better quality of hires, reduced advert spend & optimization of external hiring costs. The cost-benefit analysis results for the Global TAS initiative are shown in the Exhibit below

TAS Cost-Benefit Analysis

Allocated Heads/ Measures	Initial Initiative Outlay (INR)	Discounted cash flow years 1-5 (INR)	Cost Benefit Results (INR)
TAS Software License	-25,60,000	0	-25,60,000
TAS Software Installation	-4,20,000	0	-4,20,000
TAS Software Maintenance/ Support	0	-1,55,000	-1,55,000
External Search & Selection Costs	0	45,50,000	45,50,000
Recruitment Advertising	0	6,68,000	6,68,000
Net Present Value (NPV)			20,83,000
Internal Rate of return (IRR)			19%

Cost of Capital : 12%; Reduction in External Hire Spend, beginning in Year 2; Reduction in Advert Spend Year 2 onwards

A five year projected ROI for the TA optimization effort was also prepared by the ABC project team. The exhibit below highlights the broad outlines of the project ROI.

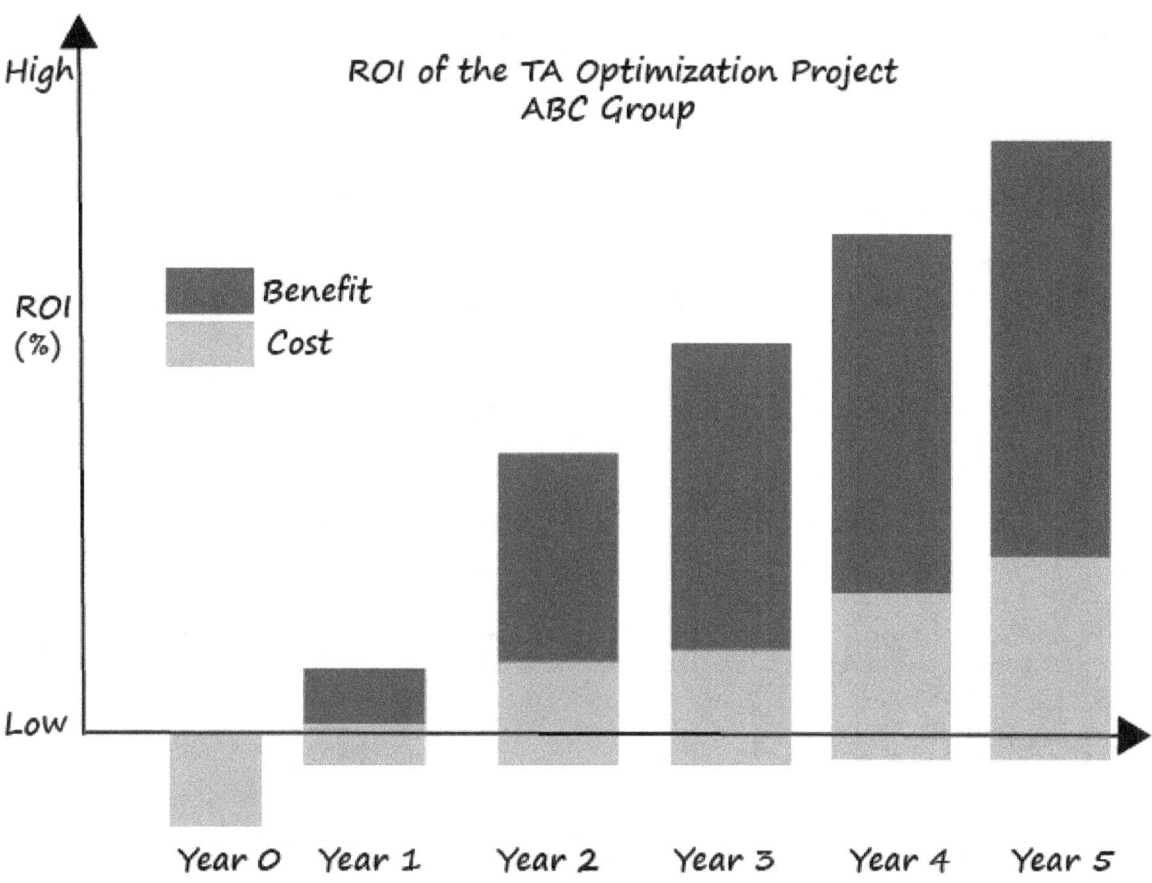

The payback was achieved at the end of Year 1 in line with the projections and the realization of positive cash flows after taking into account the technology and implementation costs upfront commenced Year 2 onwards.

12 Going Global – Localization of Talent Acquisition Strategy – ABC Group

The section here highlights salient aspects of ABC group's approach in adapting its Talent Acquisition Strategy to find and attract talent in a completely new geography. In line with its overseas expansion strategy and to take on the challenge of establishing its credibility across emerging global markets ABC group had bid and won some large Infrastructure projects in West Africa and the UAE region. The organization understood that on-boarding the right talent would be the key to solidify and strengthen its presence in these new markets. The process began with an understanding of the cultural job preferences of the target talent community leveraging on the insights provided by the _Hofstede's cultural dimensions theory_, a framework for cross-cultural communication. The Hofstede's Cultural Dimensions, a theory developed by Geert Hofstede and IBM's Personnel Department, standardizes five cultural values and provides a baseline through which different cultures can be analyzed and compared. The theory allowed ABC group to incorporate scientific evidence in its efforts to localize its talent acquisition strategy in the targeted markets.

West Africa:India

In comparing West Africa's (Gabon) cultural dimensions with those of India, refer exhibit below the TA & HR leadership team at ABC discovered that power distance is a key dimension to consider when creating a localized recruitment strategy in the region.

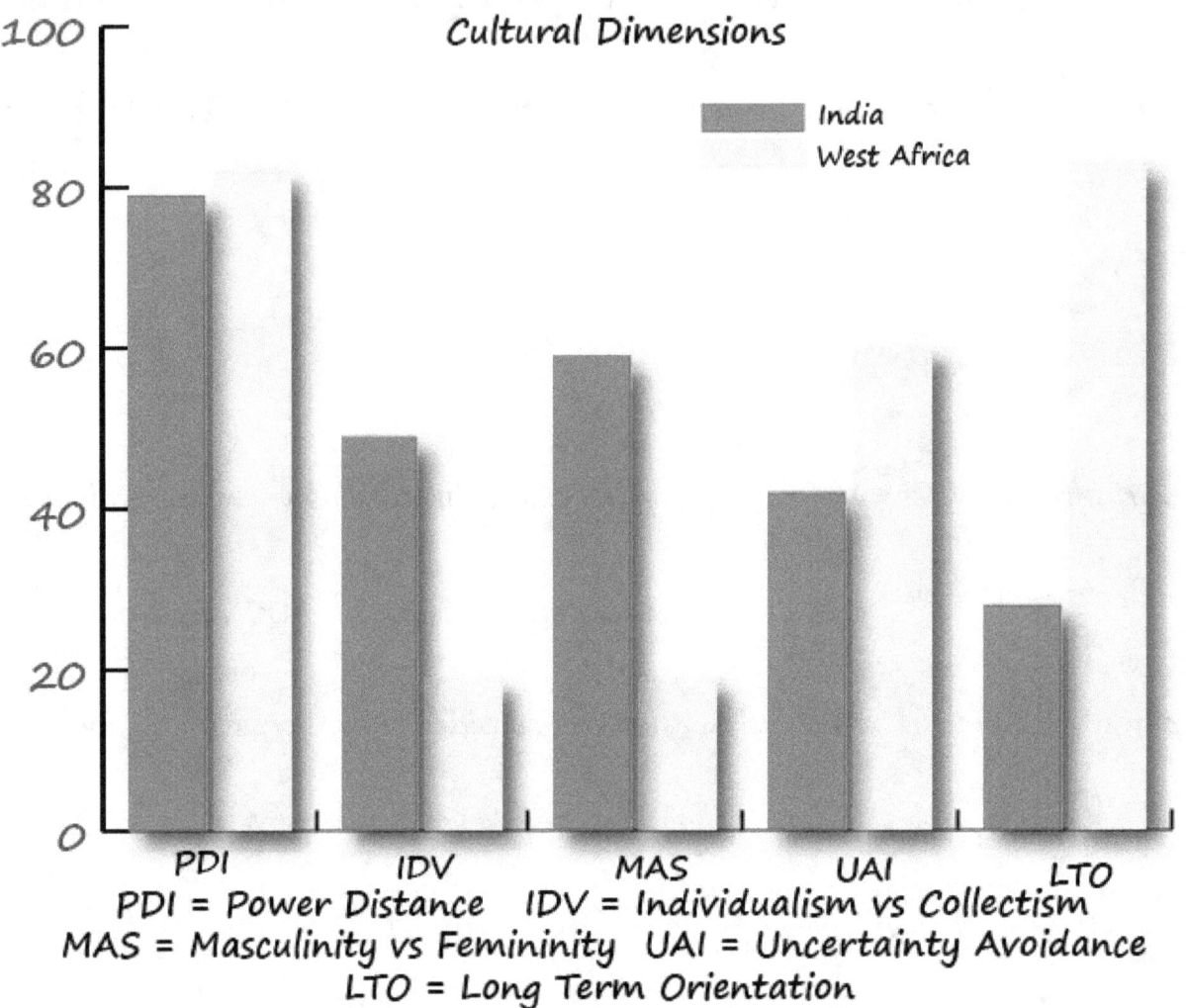

Cultural Dimensions

PDI = Power Distance   IDV = Individualism vs Collectism
MAS = Masculinity vs Femininity   UAI = Uncertainty Avoidance
LTO = Long Term Orientation

Their culture supported inequalities amongst working people and viewed

titles within the workplace as extremely important. Given this focus on

status, it was considered essential to highlight ABC group's distinctions, such

as awards and competitive rankings, and a hierarchical organization

structure based on experience and expertise of an individual. A high uncertainty avoidance (UAI) meant that the West African culture is more risk – averse than that of India. Ambiguity is viewed negatively and job-seekers prefer to weigh the facts of an employment opportunity over taking a chance. Job Seekers in the region were also focused on long-term career development and would be prone to look at an organization's overall success to gauge its stability and trajectory. Therefore, the talent outreach strategy had to be content heavy clearly delineating the ABC Employment Value Proposition.

A thoughtful employment branding strategy at the centre of its Talent Acquisition strategy helped ABC group connect with the best talent the region had to offer and underscored the importance of understanding cultural values and aspirations for organizations looking to excel at finding, attracting & retaining diverse talent within a completely new geography.

13 Epilogue

While strategy is a word that is usually associated with the future, its link to the past is no less central. Noted Danish philosopher Kierkegaard once observed, life is lived forward but understood backward. Like potters at the wheel, organizations must make sense of the past if they hope to manage the future. Only by coming to recognize the patterns that form in their own behavior do they get to know their capabilities and their potential. Thus crafting strategy, like managing craft, requires a natural synthesis of the future, present, and the past.

The Strategy Framework at the heart of ABC group's recruitment optimization effort was in essence a _Balanced Scorecard_ construct which helped look at the strategy used for value creation from four different perspectives: – please refer exhibit below – and provided TA leaders answers to four basic questions in the optimization process:

A. How do customers see us? (customer perspective)

B. What must we excel at? (operational or internal business perspective)

C. How do we look to shareholders? (financial perspective)

D. Can we continue to improve and create value? (strategic or organization learning capacity)

Talent Acquisition - Balanced Scorecard

ABC Strategy & Structure

Strategic Perspective
* Do we have the talent we need to be successful in future?
* Do we have the talent pipeline to be successful?
* How is TA helping to meet the customer service needs of our external customers?
* Are we investing in growing our
* TA capabilities?

ABC Process & Technology

Customer Perspective
* Are we viewed as a great place to work?
* How effective are our talent outreach strategies?
* Is TA viewed as an enabler in attracting & hiring top talent?
* Is TA viewed as providing effective support systems to the key stakeholders

Operational Perspective
* Are our hiring processes and support systems fostering better recruiting and selection?
* Are we using technology to improve the hiring efficiency?
* Are our hiring processes efficient and effective?

Financial Perspective
* Are our TA plans and programs competitive?
* Is our TA service delivery cost effective?
* What is our ROI in people?
* Are we managing the cost of turnover/churn?
* Does our TA function have a profit centre orientation?

ABC Employment Brand

ABC Metrics & Measures

ABC's Balanced TA Scorecard – Representative Outline

Strategic Perspective

Goals	Measures
Onboarding best talent in the market	Quality of Slate Recruiting Competition Labor Costs
Strong Employment Brand	Target Firm Hires Talent Brand Index
Continuous Innovation in all Businesses, Products & Processes	% of Hires in Strategic Roles % of Diversity Hires

Financial Perspective

Goals	Measures
Managing Turnover/ Cost of Churn	Attrition Rate New Hire Failure Rate
Improve ROI on People	Quality of Hire Cost of Vacancy Sourcing channel efficiency
Profit Centre orientation of TA	Bottom-Line Impact of Hires Bottom-Line impact of reduced CTH, TTF & RCR increased insourcing

Customer Perspective

Goals	Measures
Business Critical Partner	Hiring Manager Satisfaction Offer Acceptance Rate Time to Hire
A Great Place to Work	New Hire Satisfaction Rate Engagement Index Referral Hires

Operational Perspective

Goals	Measures
Hiring Process Excellence	Cost to Hire Time to Hire Process Cycle Time Recruiter Cost Ratio Throughput
Technology Capability & Integration	Automated tracking of pre and post hire metrics TAS Cost-Benefit Analysis

Source: Adapted from The Balanced Scorecard: Measures That Drive Performance; Robert S. Kaplan and David P. Norton

The 'balanced scorecard' served as a focal point for ABC' efforts, defining and communicating priorities to all the affected stakeholders. It provided a common vocabulary to understand both historic and emerging patterns leveraging the financial and non-financial measures.

According to Kaplan and Norton[29], the scorecard success relies on crafting clear cause – and – effect relationships across the four perspectives, creating a balance among the different measures of performance drivers and results, and communicating strategy and the processes and systems necessary to implement the strategy. **Strategy mapping** makes explicit the cause- and – effect links by which initiatives and resources – tangible and intangibles – create outcomes at the top of the scorecard. Kaplan and Norton however point out that simply building scorecard and bucketing initiatives and measures into the discrete balanced scorecard perspectives

[29] R.S. Kaplan and D.P. Norton, "The Balanced Scorecard- Measures that Drive Performance," HBR 70, no 1(1992)

without understanding the linkages is invalid. The power of strategy mapping lies in systematically and logically linking across the perspectives to create value. The **Exhibit(s) below** illustrate the value creation that was enabled by unlocking these cause- and- effect linkages in the recruitment optimization effort at ABC group. They show a logical, step-by-step connection between the talent acquisition strategic objectives (shown as ovals on the map) in the form of a cause-and-effect chain. For instance, improving performance in the objectives found in the strategic Organization Learning capacity (bottom row) enabled ABC to improve its Internal Process or Operational perspective objectives (the next row up), which in turn enabled ABC to create the desired outcomes in the Financial and Customer perspectives for its recruiting function.

Strategy Mapping - Talent Acquisition Optimization at ABC Gp

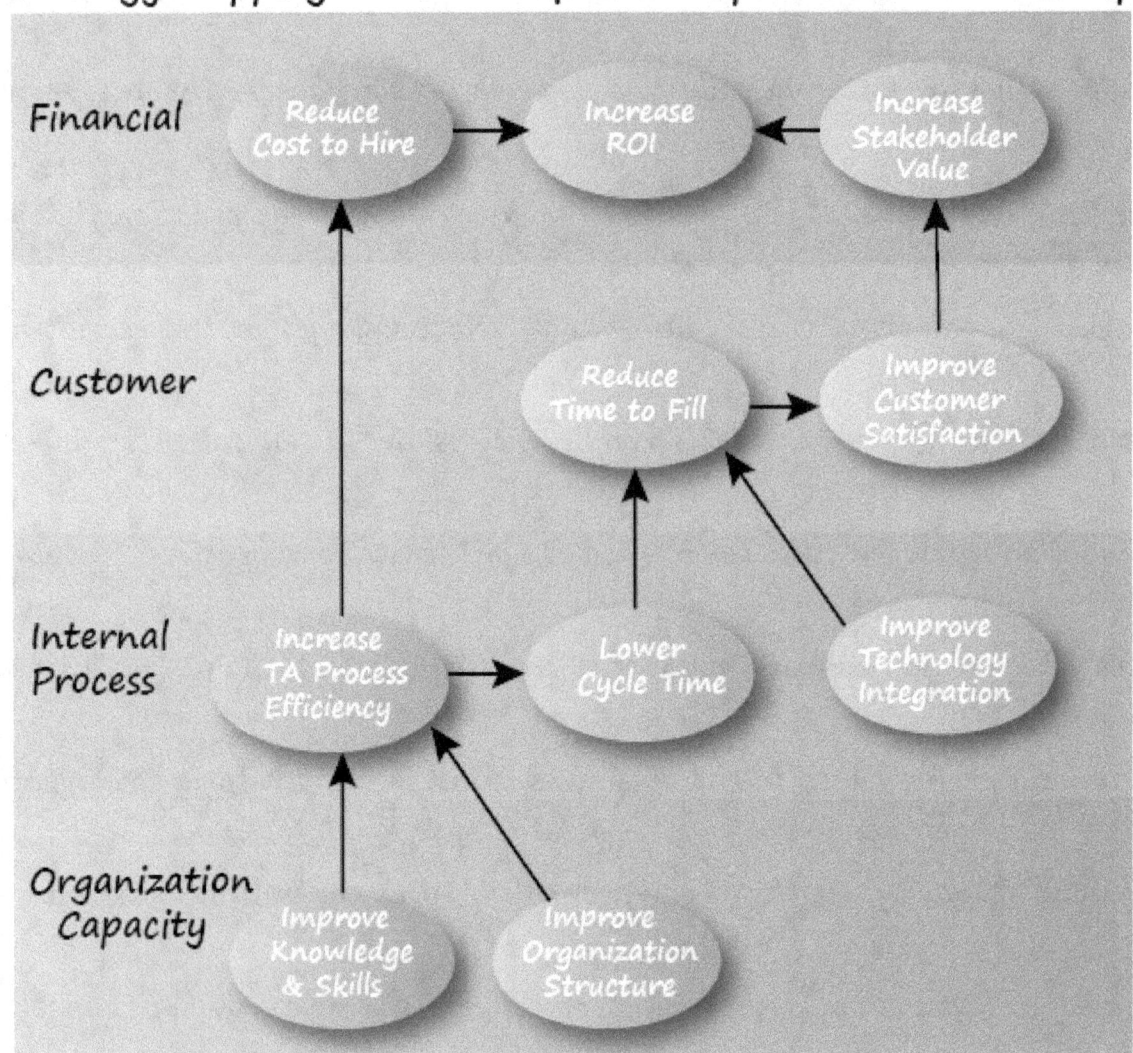

Source: Adapted from: The Institute Way: Simplify Strategic Planning & Mgmt
with the Balanced Scorecard

" The Real Opportunity for Talent Acquisition optimization was locked in the way different dimensions of the Strategic Framework (Brand, Structure, Process, Technology and metrics) interacted with each other..."

Process & Technology

Metrics & Measures

Optimization

Structure

Brand & Strategy

Source: Adapted from KPMG in India Analysis

Key Success Factors – The Mechanics Behind the Optimization

ABC' success of its TA optimization effort, in large measure, hinged around its ability to synthesize, identify, and leverage dispersed capabilities within the organization. This path to a truly game-changing TA strategy was rife with complexity and ambiguity. How can both strategy and execution be consistently superior? How can they support a culture of "one" yet enable high potentials to thrive as individuals? How can the strategy be global and local at the same time? And how can its processes endure yet be agile and constantly open to revitalization? Too many organizations end up making zero-sum decisions when faced with such challenges. ABC group didn't look at these issues as trade-offs. Rather, they saw them as inherent tensions – please refer **Exhibit below** – that had to be carefully managed and reconciled: A strategic orientation to be balanced by operational excellence; a sense of collective passion and purpose to be balanced by the need of individuals to build their careers; a global perspective to be balanced by local relevance; enduring commitments to leave room for renewal and regeneration. Skillfully managing all four of these tensions together helped them navigate the shift to a high – impact talent acquisition function.

The business impact – profiled in Chapter 7.0 – was significant and was duly corroborated by leading edge Industry Research presented in the Exhibit(s) below

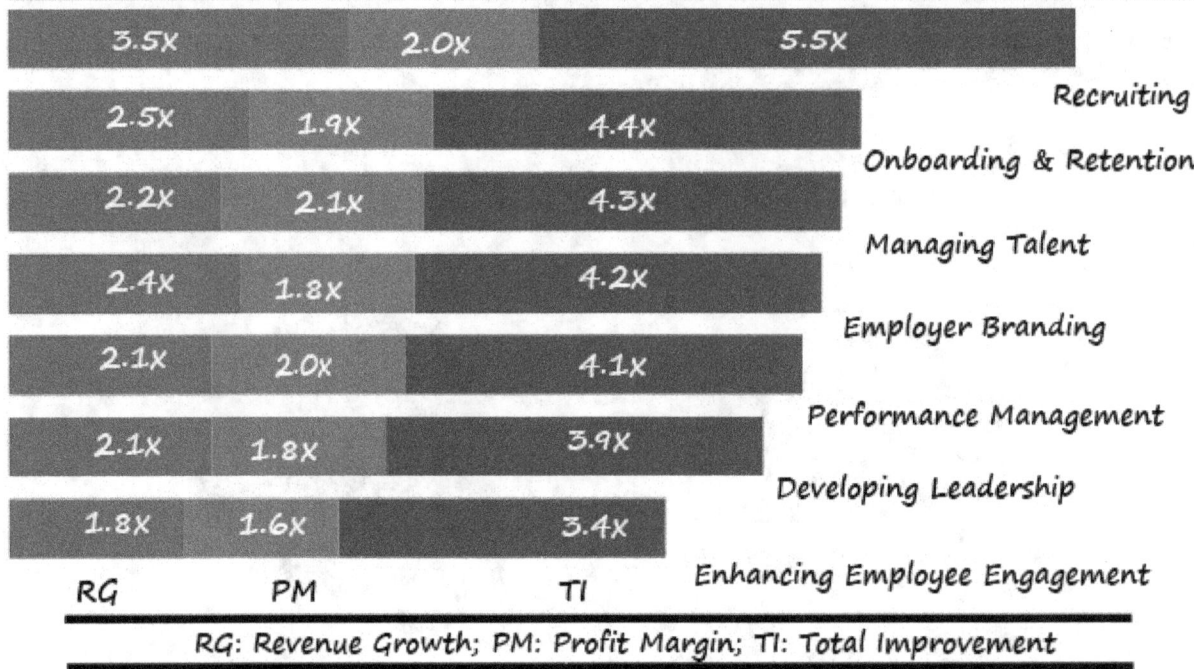

Recruiting is the most impactful HR function

Research conducted by Boston Consulting Group demonstrated that recruiting has the highest business impact on profit of any talent management function

RG	PM	TI	
3.5x	2.0x	5.5x	Recruiting
2.5x	1.9x	4.4x	Onboarding & Retention
2.2x	2.1x	4.3x	Managing Talent
2.4x	1.8x	4.2x	Employer Branding
2.1x	2.0x	4.1x	Performance Management
2.1x	1.8x	3.9x	Developing Leadership
1.8x	1.6x	3.4x	Enhancing Employee Engagement

RG: Revenue Growth; PM: Profit Margin; TI: Total Improvement

This impact of recruiting on shareholder value was also addressed in Watson Wyatt's Human Capital Index. The study showed that improving one scale point (on a 1-5 scale) in practices for recruiting and retention would yield an increase of 7.9% in an organization's market value. Unfortunately, because the budget for Talent Acquisition and mobility is an insignificant percentage of its revenue, it is often ignored. However as shown in the

242

Chart below, this budget has a huge leverage on the performance of the organization.

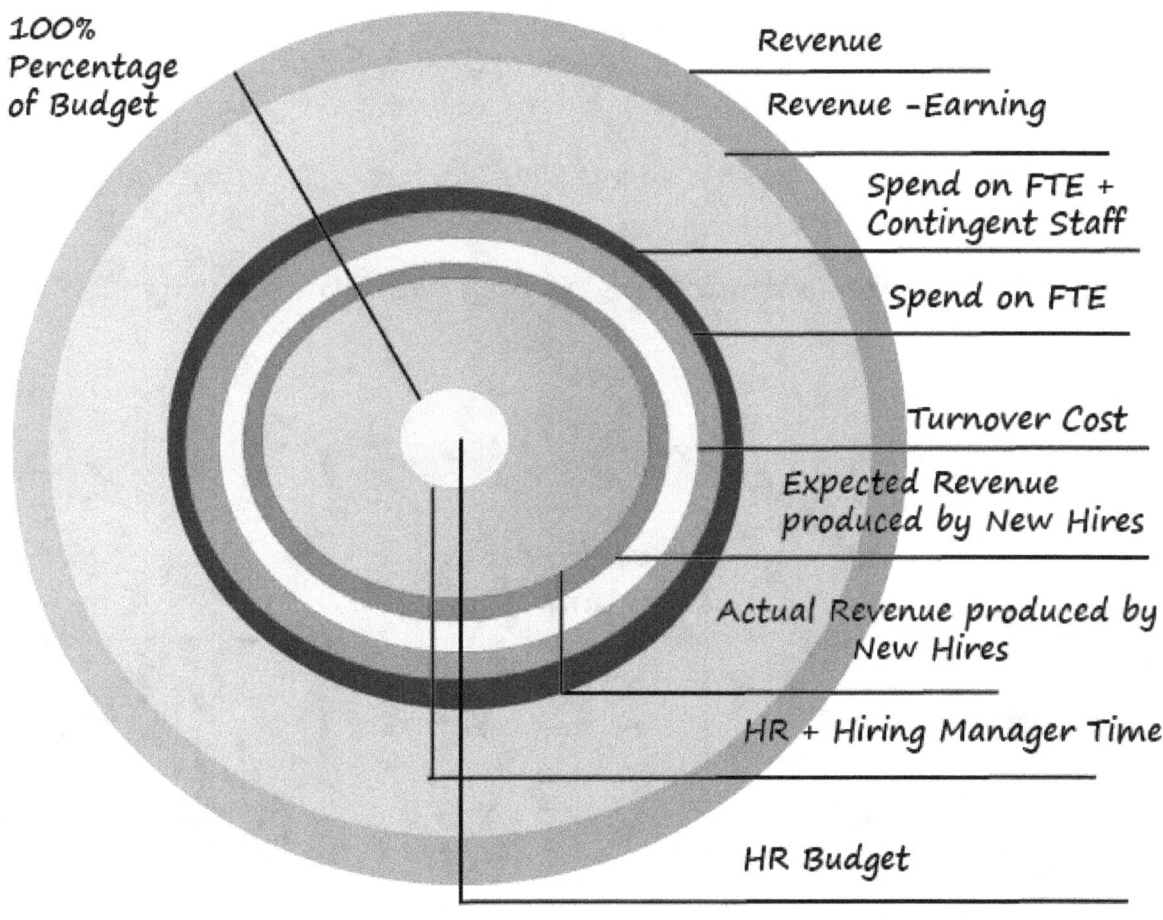

Scope of Economic Impact of Talent Acquisition on an Organization
(% of total company revenue)

100% Percentage of Budget

Revenue

Revenue -Earning

Spend on FTE + Contingent Staff

Spend on FTE

Turnover Cost

Expected Revenue produced by New Hires

Actual Revenue produced by New Hires

HR + Hiring Manager Time

HR Budget

Source: Taleo Research

Achieving such tangible business outcomes will require companies to come up with truly game-changing strategies, the ones that will lead them out of the spaces where most companies compete for talent and into the <u>Blue Ocean</u> of less (or un) contested market spaces for talent. As 2015 gets underway the business and organization pressures for finding and hiring top talent could not be greater. In many ways the recruiting function of today, as the **exhibits below** illustrate, finds parallels with wine-growing

Recruitment & Wine - Growing

"Give me wine to wash me clean of the weather -stains of cares."

Ralph Waldo Emerson

Prosperity amid climate change is the challenge for both, and for the recruitment function as for vineyards struggling with new weather patterns, this means leaving old approaches behind and finding new ways to grow

"Give me the right talent to wash me clear of all my business worries."

Hiring Manager

Recruitment has not changed in terms of a process — a vacancy needs a suitable hire. However, the landscape, tools, technology, behaviors, expectations and generations are changing all around us and continue to accelerate how organizations approach their ability to source and acquire talent. Forward looking companies such as ABC have been seizing this opportunity to move their capabilities forward and creating true competitive advantage in talent sourcing and acquisition. They are focusing on fine-tuning the fundamentals, while devoting increased time and planning to the more strategic areas of talent acquisition, including workforce planning and strategic sourcing. Their standout recruiting results comes from Blue Ocean Recruiting — game-changing strategies that elevate recruitment from a transactional, short-term focused activity to a strategic, integrated, long-term approach that optimizes their investments in people in a way that makes the competition irrelevant.

14 Bibliography

Chapter 3: The Changing Talent Acquisition Landscape – A Macro View

- The Economist, 2006, Survey: talent.'' The Economist'' from http://www.economist.com

- Price Waterhouse Coopers,2008a, The 11th Annual Global CEO Survey, PWC, New York (September, 2008)

- Claudio Araoz, Boris Groysberg and Nitin Nohria, The definitive guide to Recruiting in Good Times and Bad, Harvard Business review, May'2009.

- Ulrich D.2006. The Talent Trifecta. Workforce Management, (September 10, 2006), pp. 32-33

- The Global War for Talent, Schon Beechler, Ian C. Woodward, Journal of International Management, Fox School of Business, Temple University

- The Big Idea – 21st- Century Talent Spotting, Claudio Fernández-Aráoz, **HBR , June 2014**
- "Every Step You Take, Every Move You Make, I'll Be Watching You – Big Data and Recruiting ", by Raghav Singh; ere.net, Dec 21, 2012

Chapter 5: Talent Acquisition at ABC Group – A Historical perspective

- Laurano, Madeline. "Talent Acquisition 2013: Adapt Your Strategy or Fail", http://www.ddiworld.com/DDIWorld/media/trend-research/talentacquisition2013_tr_aberdeen.pdf?ext=.pdf

Chapter 6: A Strategic Framework for Talent Acquisition at ABC Group

- The Systems Thinker, Vol 7, No 3, Colleen P Lannon; 1996 Pegasus Communications, Inc, Cambridge, MA
- Senge, Peter M. 1990, Fifth Discipline: The Art and Practice of the Learning organization, New York
- Winning Operating Models, by David Cooper, Sanjay Dhiri and James Root;http://www.bain.com/Images/BAIN_BRIEF_Winning_operating_models.pdf
- Taleo Research White Paper – Hidden ROI of Talent Acquisition & Mobility, 2006
- "Talent Metrics that Matter", Human Capital Institute, USA
- "Make Your Company a Talent Factory", https://hbr.org/2007/06/make-your-company-a-talent-factory/ar/1
- Optimizing the organization, Subhash Khare, Tata Mc-graw Hill Publishing Company Limited (2006)

- Ulrich, D (1995), Shared Services: From vogue to value. Human Resource Planning, 18(3) 12-24

- Douglas Brown and Scott Wilson, The Black Book of Outsourcing, Wiley India Edition, 2010

- Khare S., Optimizing the Organization: Unleashing the Potential of Practices, Processes and People, Tata McGraw-Hill, 2006

- HR – How well do we measure up in the Boardroom? KPMG Thought Leadership

- Griffiths D. (2001), The Theory and Practice of Outsourcing (White Paper)

- Kai Mertins, Roland Jochem – "Quality Oriented Design of Business Processes."

- Bryan Bergeron, Essentials of Shared Services, John Wiley & Sons, Inc., 2003

- Hackett Group(n.d.) World-Class HR metrics: World class spend less, yet achieve higher effectiveness. January, 2006, www.hackettgroup.com

- Corporate Leadership Council, 2009, technology to support Integrated Talent Management.

- James Brian Quinn, IBM (A) case, in James Brian Quinn, Henry Mintzberg, and Robert M. James, *The Strategy Process: Concepts, Contexts, Cases* (Englewood Cliffs, N.J.: Prentice-Hall, forthcoming)

- Danny Miller and Peter H. Friesen, "Archetypes of Strategy Formulation," *Management Science*, May 1978, p. 921.

- *Developing a Human Resource Strategy, Wayne Brockbank, University of Michigan*
- *Jossey Bass, Organization Culture and Leadership, Edgar.H.Schein, 3rd Edition*
- *Organization Communication for Survival: Making Work, Work. Richmond, McCroskey, & McCroskey (2005)*
- *McKinsey Quarterly, "McKinsey Quarterly: Eric Schmidt on business culture, technology, and social issues", May 2011*
- *Six Sigma for Everyone by George Eckes (www.georgeeckes.com)*
- *Madeline Laurano, "Should Your organization Consider a Recruitment Centre of Excellence?" August 19, 2009, Bersin by Deloitte.*
- *Failure Modes and Effects Analysis, http://en.wikipedia.org/wiki/Failure_mode_and_effects_analysis*
- *Brockbank, W., & Ulrich, D. (2003), Competencies for the new HR, University of Michigan Business School, Global Alliance, Society for Human Resource Management*
- *Cicek I. & Ozer B. (2011), The effect of outsourcing human resource on Organizational Performance: the role of Organization Culture, International Journal of Business and Management Studies, Vol 3, No 2, 2011.*

- http://www.bersin.com/News/Details.aspx?id=15397, The New Talent Acquisition Framework
- ''Make Your Company a Talent Factory'', https://hbr.org/2007/06/make-your-company-a-talent-factory/ar/1
- ''Straight from the CEO'', G. William Dauphinais and Colin Price, Price Water House Coopers, Simon and Schuster Inc, 1998
- Adapted from 'A Question of Balance', Managing the professional services firm, David Maister, Simon & Schuster, 1997, pp. 3-9
- Adapted from 'On the Importance of Scheduling', Managing the professional services firm, David Maister, Simon & Schuster, 1997, pp. 181-184
- Adapted from ''Successful Talent Strategies'', David Sears; Amacom publication, pp. 77-79
- ''High Impact Talent Acquisition – Key Findings & Maturity Model'', Bersin by Deloitte, September, 2014
- Recruiting Roundtable, *The State of the Recruiting Function,* Corporate Executive Board (January 2006)
- Journal of Corporate Recruiting Leadership | crjournal.com | August'2007
- Robert S. Kaplan and David P. Norton, The Balanced Scorecard, Translating Strategy into Action (Boson; Harvard Business School Press, 1996)
- David Sears, Successful Talent Strategies; AMACOM 2003, p. 214

- Data, Metrics, Analytics: The Hierarchy of Knowledge, http://blog.smashfly.com/2014/11/20/data-metrics-analytics-the-hierarchy-of-knowledge/
- Hammer, M. (1990), "Reengineering Work; Don't Automate, Obliterate," HBR, July/August, pp. 104-112
- Hammer, M., Champy. J., (1993), "Reengineering the Corporation: A Manifesto for Business Revolution.", Harper Collins, London
- 2006, Mary B. Young: Strategic Workforce Planning, The Conference Board
- 2007, Ann Cotton, Seven Steps of Effective Workforce Planning, Human Capital Management Series
- Brian E. Becker, Mark A. Huselid, and Dave Ulrich, The HR Scorecard: Linking People, Strategy, and Performance (HBS Press, 2001), pp.94-95

Chapter 11: Results Produced by the ABC Group Recruiting Team

- Corporate Recruiting Reports, http://www.staffing.org/documents/07_CostandTimeReportLookInside.pdf

- Hofstede's Cultural Dimensions Theory: http://geert-hofstede.com/applications.html
- Hofstede, Geert(1980), Culture's consequences: International Differences in Work — Related Values. Beverly Hills, CA; Sage Applications
- Moroko, L., & Uncles, M.D. Characteristics of Successful Employer Brands. Journal of Brand Management, 16(3), 160-175
- Ma, R., & Allen, D.G., Recruiting across cultures: A Value based model of recruitment, Human Resource Management Review (2009), doi: 10.1016/j.hrmr.2009.03.001
- Hofstede, G. (1991). Cultures and organizations: Software of the mind. London: McGraw-Hill
- Ployhart, R.E. (2006). Staffing in the 21st century: New Challenges and Strategic Opportunities. Journal of Management, 32(6), pp.868-897

Epilogue

- Robert S. Kaplan and David P. Norton, The Balanced Scorecard, Translating Strategy into Action (Boston: Harvard Business School Press, 1996).

15 Glossary

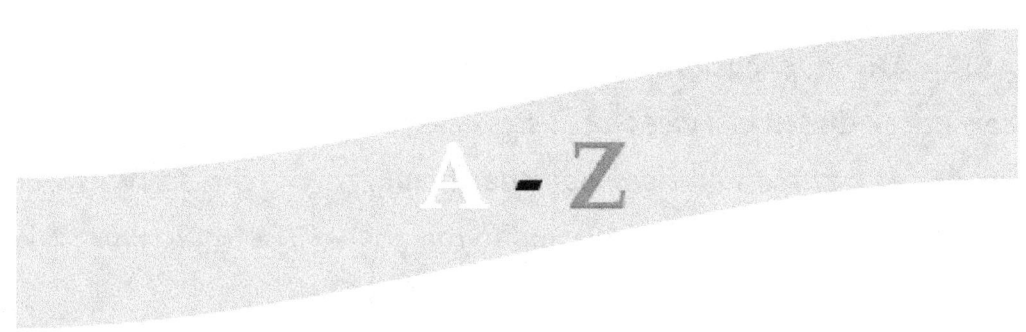

A

Analytics: The method of logical analysis — a careful study of something to learn about its parts, what they do, and how they relate to each other. It provides an explanation of the nature and meaning of something. Analytics are intangible, future-focused in an attempt to predict possible outcomes and designed to provide insights to enable informed decision making.

API: An application Programming Interface (API) is a set of routines, protocols, and tools for building software applications.. It enables one application to talk to another. In the context of recruitments it provides a seamless integration of the application tracking systems with external applications, candidate audiences and vendors.

ATS: Application Tracking System (ATS) is a software application used to manage the talent acquisition process. Originally designed as resume collection systems, over time, these systems evolved into workflow management systems enabling recruiters to put job postings online, collect & filter resumes, and assess them for fit. Modern applicant-tracking systems are cloud enabled and more resemble an 'integration platform' that not only track & manage resumes but also store valuable data about the entire talent acquisition process.

ASP: An application service provider (ASP) is a business providing computer-based services o customers over a remote network. In the ASP model, the customer does not specifically 'own' the software but 'rents' it — and the software company runs it for them. The modernized version of ASP is also called "Software as a Service" (SaaS).

Assessments: An "assessment" is a test or form of evaluation that measures skills, competencies, knowledge, and behavioural traits. Many types of assessments tools are used in the recruitment process that can be leveraged to determine job fit, uncover personality attributes, and cultural fit. Some leading providers of assessments tools and services include SHL, DDI, CPP, Korn Ferry, and Hogan Assessments among others.

B

Balanced Scorecard: The balanced scorecard (BSC) is a strategy performance management tool which leverages both financial and non-financial measures in assessing organization and /or functional performance. It breaks business strategy into four levels of goals: financial, customer, process, and people. By combining perspectives, the balanced scorecard helps unlock the real value underlying the many interrelationships across these four levels.

Big Data: The term 'Big Data' refers to large and complex data sets that cannot be processed using traditional data processing applications. The term often refers to the use of predictive analytics or other advanced methods to extract value from data and is characterised by the 4Vs: Volume, Velocity, Veracity and Variety.

Blue Ocean Strategy: A perspective on strategy formulation and execution created by INSEAD professors W. Chan Kim and Renee Mauborgne. The logic behind blue ocean strategy parts with traditional models focused on competing in existing market space to one based on systematically creating "blue oceans" of uncontested market space ripe for growth. This strategy outlook aligns the whole system of a company's activities in pursuit of value and cost differentiation.

C

Candidate: A candidate is anyone who engages with an employer brand while exploring the possibility of a new job, now or in the future, who hasn't applied, or is no longer being considered for a position.

Candidate Experience: The collective result of all the interactions a candidate has with an employer brand during the recruitment marketing and the hiring process.

Candidate Pools: Also referred to as a "Talent Pool", they are generated from the process of engaging and grouping candidates by interest levels, background, skills and experiences.

Candidate Audiences: Segmented pool of candidates targeted by an organization through appropriate employer branding and content strategies with the ultimate objective of attracting, engaging and on-boarding them. The accent is on cultivating a long-term relationship capital with the right candidates.

Cascading Goals: A process of adopting goals at different levels within a company to ensure alignment between the organization's objectives, and employees' activities and goals.

Causal Model: An abstract model that describes the causal mechanisms of a system. The model must express more than correlation because correlation does not imply causation.

Causal Diagram: A graphical tool that enables the visualization of causal relationships between variables in a causal model.

Causal Loop Diagram: A "causal loop diagram" (CLD) is a causal diagram that aids in visualizing how different variables in a system are interrelated. The diagram consists of a st of nodes and edges. Nodes represent the variables and edges are the links that that represent a connection or relation between the two variables. It is a method of analysis used to develop an understanding of complex systems.

Center of Excellence: A "Center of Excellence" (COE) refers to a shared facility, corporate structure or a team that provides leadership, evangelization, best practices, research, support and/or training for a focus area. It is also variously called as "Competency Centre" or "Capability Center". In the recruiting context, organizations create a COE based on their individual hiring needs. Key drivers could include: standardization of recruitment processes and metrics, workforce planning, employer branding, to name a few.

Change Management: The term refers to a broad discipline of programs, processes, and tools that drive organizational change. It is an approach to transitioning individuals, teams, and organizations to a desired future state.

Cloud Computing: The practice of using a network of remote servers hosted on the internet to store, manage, and process data rather than a local server or a personal computer. It relies on sharing of resources to achieve coherence and economies of scale.

Cloud Recruiting: The concept of outsourcing recruiting using a data driven, highly predictive process utilizing the collective intelligence of successful hires, the expanded candidate reach of crowdsourcing through known and nknown social connections allowing recruiting capacity to scale on-demand in a highly capital and resource efficient manner leveraging software as a service (SaaS) in a cloud computing model

Crowdsourcing: "Crowdsourcing" is a practice of obtaining needed services, ideas, or content by soliciting contributions from a large group people, and especially from an online community or the internet, rather than from traditional employees or suppliers.

Competency: A "competency" is a measurable characteristic of a person that is related to success at work. It may be a behavioral skill, a technical skill, an attribute (such as intelligence), or an attitude (such as optimism)

Content Strategy: Creating and curating compelling content and messaging to attract and engage with prospective talent specific to the business context of an organization. Tools could include infographics, recruiting micro-sites, blogs, videos, career sites, among others.

Customer Relationship Management: It is a system for managing an organization's interactions with present and future customers. It often involves using technology to organize, automate and synchronize sales, marketing, customer service and support. Modern Applicant Tracking Systems often resemble a Customer Relationship Management (CRM) system, in that they focus on tracking the activities associated with a particular with a particular performed by the user.

D

Data Science: In general terms, data science is the extraction of knowledge from data. It draws upon techniques and theories from multiple disciplines such as mathematics, statistics, and information technology. Data Science techniques affect research in many domains, including healthcare, social sciences and now Human Resources.

Datafication: is a modern technological trend turning an existing business into a "data business" and transforming this information into new forms of value. In HR it refers to our increasing ability to use Talent Analytics to understand more about people, HR practices and processes and external demographics.

E

Employer Branding: Activities that help to uncover, articulate and define a company's image, culture, key differentiators, reputation, and products and services. It is the image of an organization as a 'great place to work' in the mind of current employees and key stakeholders in the external market. The process of employer branding is concerned with talent attraction, engagement and retention strategies deployed to enhance an organization's employer brand.

Engagement Strategy: An organization's strategy for engaging with its critical talent with the end objective of aligning the individual and the business goals.

F

Farming: A Talent pipelining concept which seeks to proactively identify and establish relationships with top talent in the marketplace well in advance of an actual hiring need.

Flight Risk: Flight risk refers to the degree to which a top performing employee appears ready to leave current employment, presumably for a better opportunity elsewhere.

G

Gamification: The use of game thinking and game mechanics in non-game contexts to engage users in problem solving. Applied to talent acquisition, it involves the use of games, simulations and other multi-media rich applications in hiring, selection, and assessment processes.

Generation-Y: Also known as "Millennials", they are individuals who were born between 1981 and 2000, and are culturally thought to be confident, impatient, socially conscious and technology –savvy.

Groupthink: "Groupthink" is a psychological phenomenon that occurs within a group of people, in which the desire for harmony or conformity in the group results in an irrational or dysfunctional decision-making outcomes.

H

High Potential or HiPo: A "high potential" employee is an individual who has been identified as having the potential, ability, and the aspiration for successive leadership positions within the company. Often, these employees are identified as part of a succession plan and are referred to as 'HiPos".

Hiring & On-boarding: A strategic process of integrating the new hires into a company's workplace environment through forms management, tasks management and socialization in the company culture.

Human Capital: The total knowledge, skills and capabilities of an organization's workforce.

I

Internal Mobility: "Internal Mobility" or talent mobility is a dynamic internal process for moving talent across roles – leadership, operational and professional levels. To achieve internal mobility, companies must adopt the principles of succession management at all ranks; provide transparent discussion of skills and development, as well as organizational needs; and focus on development across critical talent pools, based on business needs.

Interoperability: The ability of making systems and organizations work together.

J

Job Fit: "Job Fit" refers to the assessment of current knowledge skills, competencies and other key attributes of an individual against the requirements of a specific role.

Just-in-Time: A lean concept, "Just-in-Time" (JIT) is founded on the principle of continuous reduction of all inventory, while satisfying changing market demand with shorter lead times and production. Applying this concept to talent identification and acquisition, JIT recruiting is a pull based strategy of providing hiring managers with the right candidates at the right place with the right skills at the right place.

K

Key Performance Indicator: A "key performance indicator" (KPI) is a quantifiable measure of success that reflects the critical success factors of a department, project or business unit.

Kaizen: A Japanese term for "continuous improvement". When applied to the workplace, kaizen refers to activities that continually improve all functions. By improving standardized activities & processes, kaizen aims to eliminate waste resulting in overall improvement in productivity.

L

Leadership Pipeline: "leadership pipeline" refers to an organization's need to have a ready pool of talent across levels to support its growth and expansion needs.

Lean: A process improvement methodology that focuses on maximizing process velocity by reducing waste or non value-added activities. Lean operation principles are derived from the lean manufacturing practices but as lean deals with production system from a pure process point of view, and not a hardware point of view, its principles can be readily applied to improve the efficiency and velocity of all business processes including recruitment.

M

Metric: A "metric" is a standard of measure based on historical data points. They are tangible in nature and derived by trending and analysing the data captured on an ongoing basis. Commonly used metrics in recruitment include: cost per hire, time to fill, source of hire, candidate drop-off rate, among others.

Muda: "Muda" is a Japanese word meaning waste. It refers to any activity in a process that does not add value from the customer perspective. There are seven categories of waste identified in Muda which can be targeted for elimination and improve the value proposition to the customer.

N

Nine Box Grid: A "nine-box grid" is a matrix tool used to evaluate and plot a company's talent pool based on two factors: performance and potential. They are actively used during a talent review process and aid in the discussion of employee strengths and development needs to shoulder key leadership roles.

O

On-boarding: "On-boarding" also known as organizational socialization refers to the process of hiring, orienting and integrating new employees into their roles and into the organization's culture.

Optimization: A process to ensure effective and efficient deployment of existing resources for capability maximization. It is the result of interplay between utilization, efficiency and effectiveness

Organization Culture: "Organization Culture" is the most central aspect of organizational capability. It represents the collective mindset of the company – shared ways of thinking or shared cognitive patterns. It defines the way people behave, and it also determines what information people will accept, interpret accurately, and adopt as useful knowledge.

Organization Maturity: It is the level of organization's readiness and experience in relation to people, processes, technologies and consistent measurement practices.

Outsourcing: "Outsourcing" is contracting out a business function or process to a third party organization.

P

Parsing: "parsing" refers to the process of electronically identifying specific phrases or words within a document, and assigning meaning to them. For instance, in talent acquisition, the technology allows the recruiters to electronically gather, store and organize information contained in the resumes. The information so formatted is easily searchable using keywords and phrases. However it is a software searching process and often error prone.

Prehire Assessment: "Pre-hire Assessments" are scientific tools used to evaluate whether a person has the right skills to perform a job in terms of knowledge, skills, behaviour, and cultural fit.

Pugh Matrix: A decision-matrix method, the Pugh method is a quantitative technique used to rank the multi-dimensional options of an option set. A lean six sigma tool, its application as a scoring matrix can be variously applied in recruitments to rank vendor options, hiring candidate options or any other set of multidimensional entities.

Q

Quality Functional Deployment: Quality function deployment (QFD) is a structured methodology and mathematical lean six sigma tool used to identify and quantify customer needs (VOC) into key quantitative parameters. It helps to prioritize actions to improve a process or product in alignment with customer expectations.

R

Recruiting: The tactical process of attracting, selecting and on-boarding candidates; either permanent or temporary.

RPO: "Recruitment Process Outsourcing" (RPO) is a form of business process outsourcing (BPO) where an employer transfers all or part of its recruitment activities to an external service provider. A true RPO solutions provider manages the entire recruiting process from job profiling through the on-boarding of the new hire, including the people, process and technology intervention.

S

Saas Delivery Model: A delivery model where the vendor hosts and operates the technology platform at its facility. It is sometimes referred to as "on-demand software" and is typically assessed by users using a _thin client_ via a web browser. Cloud-based recruiting and application tracking software are being increasingly leveraged by organizations using a SaaS delivery model.

Screening & Assessment: Tools and technology that enable organizations to evaluate if a candidate has the right skills to perform a job.

Semantic Search: A data searching technique that seeks to improve search accuracy by understanding searcher intent and contextual meaning of terms as they appear in the searchable database. When sourcing candidates, semantic search can be achieved at the conceptual level when a search for a specific term (e.g., java) also yields matches on related terms (e.g., J2EE, EJB, servlets) – words that are related conceptually.

Shared Services Model: A business model which enables resources to be leveraged across the entire organization. A "shared-services organization" acts as an internal consulting group that provides a menu of well-defined services to line managers and line training groups. This necessitates shared accountability of results by the unit from where the work is migrated to the provider. The provider unit ensures the agreed results are delivered based on defined measures (KPI's, cost, quality etc.)

SIPOC: A SIPOC (Suppliers, Inputs, Process, Output, Customers) is a high level process map that identifies the potential gaps (deficiencies) between what a process expects from its suppliers and what customers expect from the process, thus defining the scope of the process improvement activities.

Six Sigma: "Six Sigma" is a disciplined, data-driven approach and methodology for eliminating defects and reducing process variance. The fundamental objective of the Six Sigma methodology is the implementation of a measurement-based strategy that focuses on process improvement and variation reduction through the application of Six Sigma improvement projects

Social Media: "Social Media" is an umbrella term for using the computer-mediated communication channels as new forms of media It refers to tools such as blogs, microblogs, wikis, podcasting and video/media libraries.

Social Networking: Social networking represents the use of person-to-person networking approaches that facilitate collaboration, learning, knowledge sharing and organization communication. It leverages the use of web tools for individuals to post profile information, share comments, collaborate, and join groups, communities.

Social Recruiting: "Social Recruiting" is recruiting candidates by using social platforms as talent databases or for advertising. Some popular social media channels used for recruiting include LinkedIn, Facebook, Twitter, XING, Google+.

Supply chain: A "supply chain" is a system of organizations, people, activities, information, and resources involved in moving a product or service from supplier to customer. Conventional supply chain activities transform natural resources, raw materials and components to a finished product that is delivered to a customer.

Staffing Supply Chain: Similar to a supply chain A "Staffing Supply Chain" transforms relationships and data (ad responses, resumes, social networking profiles etc.) into candidates that are delivered to hiring managers.

Staffing Plan: A staffing plan identifies the necessary human resources for delivering on the organization's goals, projects and commitments.

Systems Thinking: "Systems Thinking" is the process of understanding how things, regarded as systems, influence one another within a whole. It is an approach to problem solving that is based on the belief that the component parts of a system can best be understood in the context of relationships with each other and with other systems, rather than in isolation.

T

Talent: According to McKinsey, talent is the "sum of a person's abilities, his or her intrinsic gifts, skills, knowledge, experience, intelligence, judgment, attitude, character and drive. It also included his or her ability to learn and grow."

Talent Acquisition: "Talent Acquisition" is a strategic approach to identifying, attracting, and on-boarding top talent.

Talent Analytics: Talent Analytics refers to the analysis of talent related data for business decision making. These data points could include: demographic data, performance data, job history, compensation, mobility, assessment, training, and more. This data can be correlated and matched to many different types of business data to help companies understand profiles and behaviours which create high performance.

V

Value Stream Mapping: "Value Stream Mapping" is a lean management method for analyzing A lean process tool, value stream mapping is a fundamental tool to identify waste, reduce process cycle times, and implement process improvement.

W

Web 2.0: "Web 2.0" refers to a second generation of web based communities and hosted services (such as social networking sites, wikis, blogs, podcasts, RSS feeds, application programming interfaces), that aim to facilitate creativity, collaboration and sharing between users.

Workforce Planning: "Workforce Planning" is a process by which an organization anticipates and meets its business talent needs. Workforce planning enables evidence based workforce development strategies.

If you enjoyed this book or received value from it in any way, then I'd like to ask you for a favour: would you be kind enough to leave a review for this book on Amazon? It'd be greatly appreciated!

Click here to leave a review on Amazon.com

www.ingramcontent.com/pod-product-compliance
Lightning Source LLC
Chambersburg PA
CBHW080801180526
45168CB00006B/2291